SPECTRUM®
MATH

Kindergarten

CREDITS
Editor: Hailey Scragg
Cover Design: J.J. Giddings, Nick Pearson, Lynne Schwaner
Interior Design: J.J. Giddings
Illustrations: Nick Pearson, Robin Krantz, J.J. Giddings, Lynne Schwaner

Spectrum®
An imprint of Carson Dellosa Education
PO Box 35665
Greensboro, NC 27425 USA

Printed in the USA • All rights reserved.
ISBN 978-1-4838-7143-1
01-1062412735

Table of Contents Kindergarten

Table of Contents Kindergarten

Spectrum Introduction •••••••••••••••••••••••••••••••••••

For more than 20 years, Spectrum® workbooks have been the solution for helping students meet and exceed learning goals. Each title in the Spectrum workbook series offers grade-appropriate instruction and reinforcement in an effective sequence for learning success.

Spectrum partners with you in supporting your student's educational journey every step of the way! This book will help them navigate kindergarten math and will give you the support you need to make sure they learn everything they need to know. Inside you will find:

Chapter Introductions •••••••••••••••••••••••••••••••••••

These introductions provide useful information about the chapter. They may include:

● **Helpful Definitions**
These terms either appear in the chapter or are important for the skills being taught.

● **Tools and Tips**
Tools and tips to support and reinforce skills are explained here.

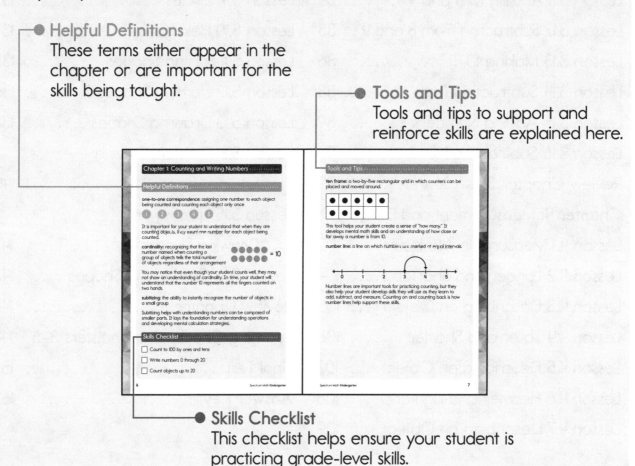

● **Skills Checklist**
This checklist helps ensure your student is practicing grade-level skills.

Lessons

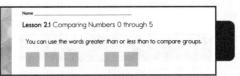

These pages begin with a definition, step-by-step instructions where needed, and examples, followed by independent practice.

Enrichment

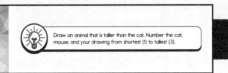

These problems appear throughout the book. They allow your student to dig deeper and apply the skill they learned in a different way than it is practiced on the page. The two types of problems will ask your student to think critically 💡 and explain reasoning 💬.

Chapter Reviews

These end-of-chapter reviews go over the skills learned within each chapter and can be used to gauge your student's progress.

Learning Checkpoints

These reviews break up the book into halfway points to prepare your student for the final test.

Final Test

This test covers the skills learned in the book. Use this comprehensive test to assess what your student has learned and to identify what they still need to work on.

Answer Key

The answers to the lessons, reviews, and tests are provided in an answer key.

Chapter 1: Counting and Writing Numbers

Helpful Definitions

one-to-one correspondence: assigning one number to each object being counted and counting each object only once

It is important for your student to understand that when they are counting objects, they count one number for each object being counted.

cardinality: recognizing that the last number named when counting a group of objects tells the total number of objects regardless of their arrangement

 = 10

You may notice that even though your student counts well, they may not show an understanding of cardinality. In time, your student will understand that the number 10 represents all the fingers counted on two hands.

subitizing: the ability to instantly recognize the number of objects in a small group

Subitizing helps with understanding numbers can be composed of smaller parts. It lays the foundation for understanding operations and developing mental calculation strategies.

Skills Checklist

☐ Count to 100 by ones and tens

☐ Write numbers 0 through 20

☐ Count objects up to 20

ten frame: a two-by-five rectangular grid in which counters can be placed and moved around.

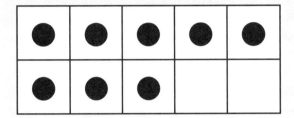

This tool helps your student create a sense of "how many." It develops mental math skills and an understanding of how close or far away a number is from 10.

number line: a line on which numbers are marked at equal intervals

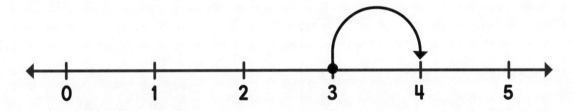

Number lines are important tools for practicing counting, but they also help your student develop skills they will use as they learn to add, subtract, and measure. Counting on and counting back is how number lines help support these skills.

Lesson 1.1 Counting 0, 1, and 2

zero	one	two
0	1	2

Count the number of objects out loud. Then, circle the correct number.

0 1 2   0 1 2

0 1 2   0 1 2

Lesson 1.2 Writing 0, 1, and 2

Count the number of objects out loud. Trace the number. Write the number.

Lesson 1.3 Counting 3 and 4

Circle the objects in each group to match the given number. Then, write the number.

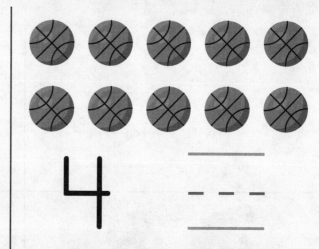

3 _ _ _ _

4 _ _ _ _

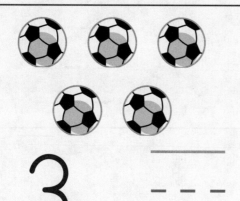

3 _ _ _ _

4 _ _ _ _

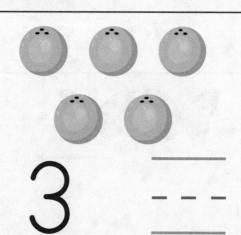

3 _ _ _ _

4 _ _ _ _

Name _____

Lesson 1.4 Writing 3 and 4

Count the number of objects out loud. Trace the number. Write the number.

Lesson 1.5 Counting 0 through 4

zero 0	one 1	two 2	three 3	four 4

Circle the number.

0   1   2   3   4

0   1   2   3   4

0   1   2   3   4

0   1   2   3   4

0   1   2   3   4

0   1   2   3   4

Lesson 1.6 Counting 0 through 5

Count the number of objects in each group out loud. Then, circle the correct number.

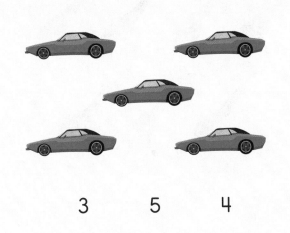

3   5   4

2   3   1

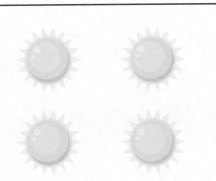

4   3   5

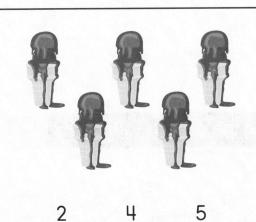

2   4   5

3   4   1

2   5   3

Lesson 1.7 Writing 5

Circle the objects to make 5. Trace the number. Write the number.

Color the objects to make 5.

Name _____

Lesson 1.8 Counting On: 0 through 5

A number line can help with counting. This number line starts at 0 and counts by ones up to 5.

Find the number that comes after **3**.

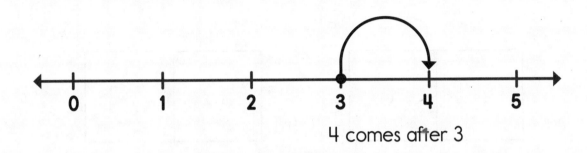

4 comes after 3

Use the number line to write the numbers that come after.

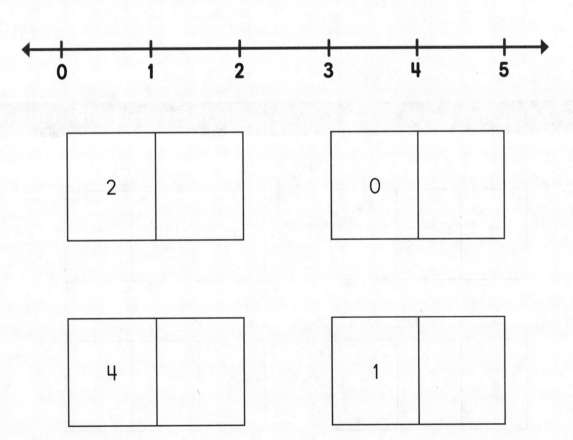

Lesson 1.8 Counting On: 0 through 5

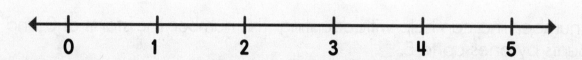

Use the number line to help you write the numbers that come before.

	1

	3

	5

	2

Use the number line to help you write the numbers that come between.

2		4

0		2

1		3

3		5

Lesson 1.9 Counting 6 and 7

Count the number of objects in each group out loud. Then, circle the correct number.

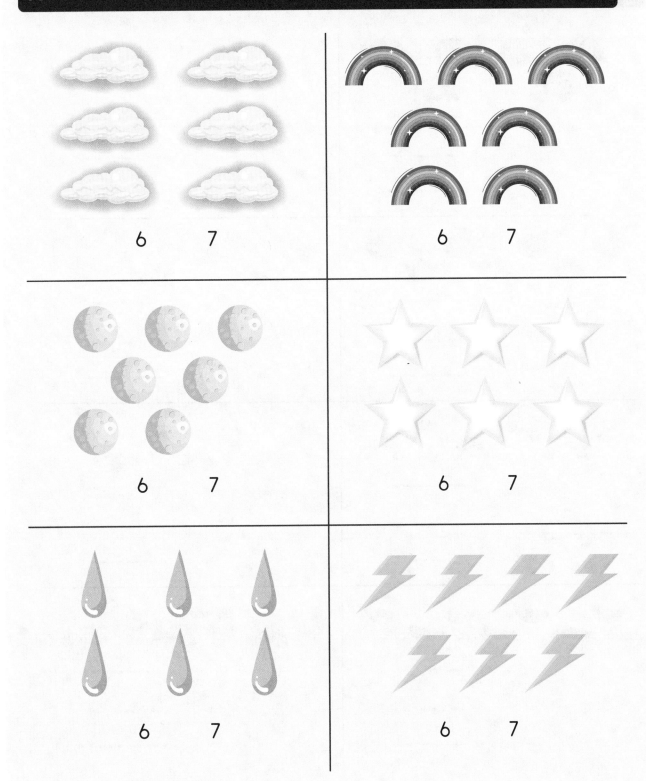

6   7

6   7

6   7

6   7

6   7

6   7

Lesson 1.10 Writing 6 and 7

Count the number of objects in each group out loud. Trace the number. Write the number.

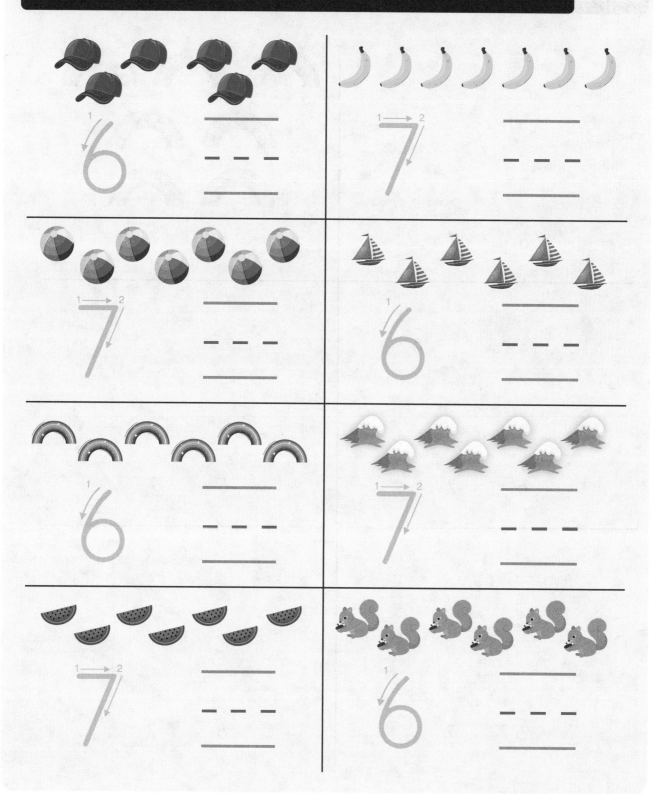

Lesson 1.11 Counting 5 through 7

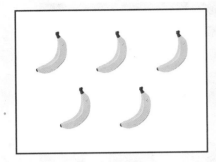
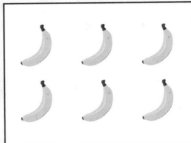
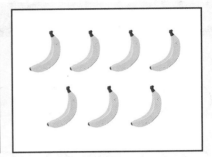

five   six   seven
5   6   7

Circle the number.

5   6   7

5   6   7

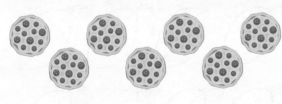

5   6   7

5   6   7

5   6   7

5   6   7

Lesson 1.12 Counting 8 and 9

Circle the objects to make the given number. Then, write the number.

Color the objects to make the given number.

Lesson 1.13 Writing 8 and 9

Count the number of objects in each group out loud. Trace the number. Write the number.

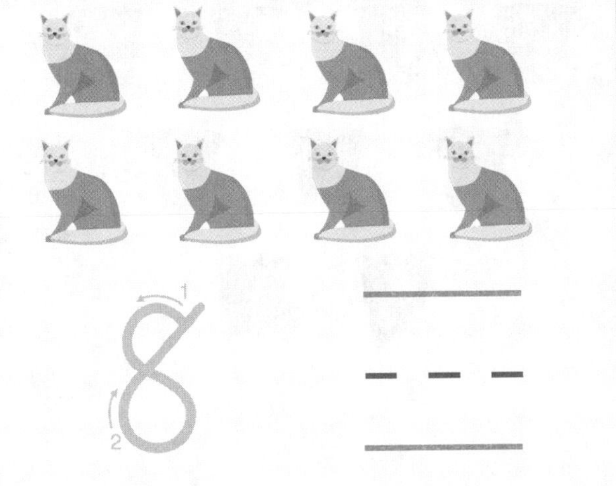

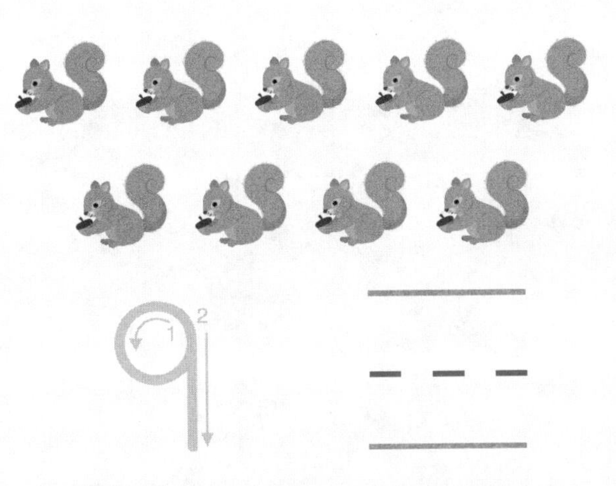

8

9

9

8

8

9

Lesson 1.14 Counting 5 through 10

Count the number of objects in each group out loud. Then, circle the correct number.

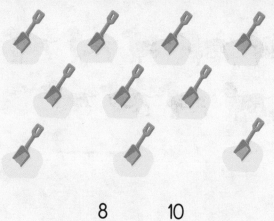

8   10

7   9

7   6

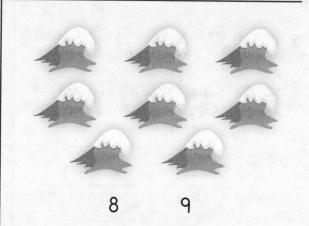

8   9

5   6

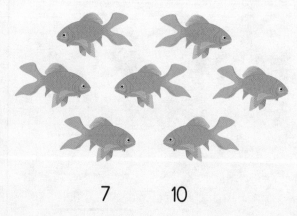

7   10

Lesson 1.15 Writing 10

Cross out the extra objects in each group to make 10. Trace the number. Write the number. The first one has been done for you.

Lesson 1.16 Counting 8 through 10

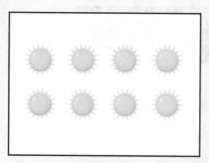 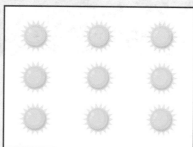 

eight	nine	ten
8	9	10

Circle the number.

8   9   10

8   9   10

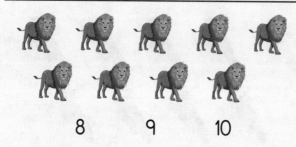

8   9   10

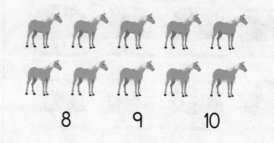

8   9   10

 Draw 8 circles. Touch and count the circles. Write the number 8.

_____

- - - -

_____

Lesson 1.17 Counting 0 through 10

Cut out the numbers. Glue the numbers in order in the boxes. Say the numbers in order as you count them.

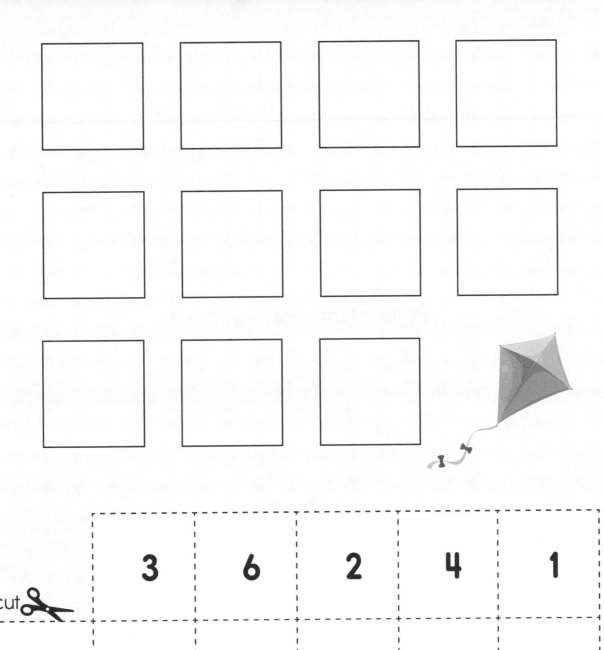

cut ✂

| 3 | 6 | 2 | 4 | 1 |
| 8 | 5 | 9 | 7 | 10 | 0 |

Page intentionally left blank.

Lesson 1.18 Counting On: 0 through 10

A **ten frame** helps you count. It has 10 spaces: 5 on the top and 5 on the bottom. Cut out the counters to complete the ten frame activities.

This ten frame shows 8. Use the counters to show 10.

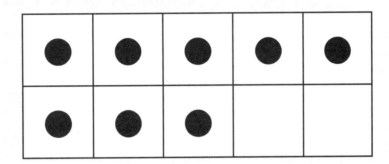

This ten frame shows 4. Use the counters to show 7.

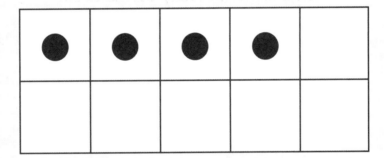

How many counters did you add to each ten frame?

ten frame
with 8 counters _____

ten frame
with 4 counters _____

✂ cut

Page intentionally left blank.

Lesson 1.19 Counting and Writing 0 through 10

Count how many. Write the number.

Lesson 1.19 Counting and Writing 0 through 10

Count how many. Write the number.

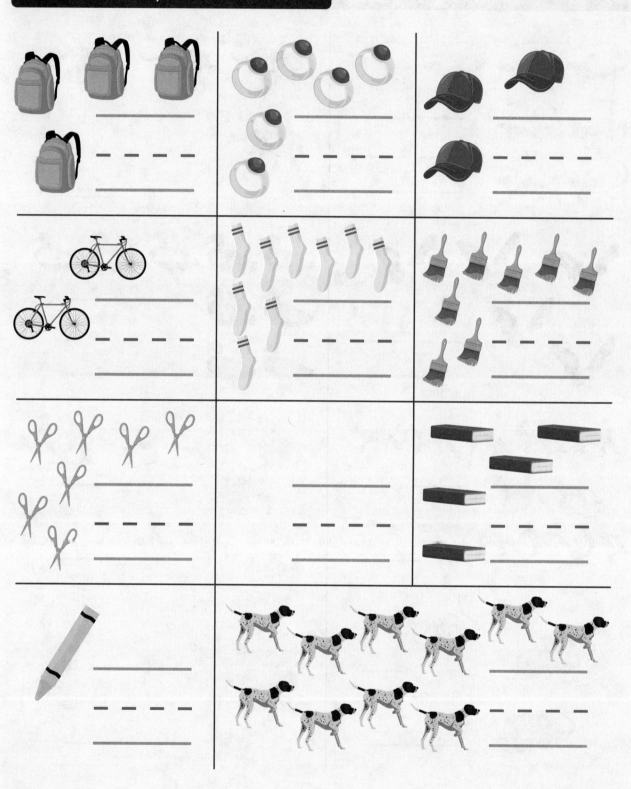

Lesson 1.19 Counting and Writing 0 through 10

Count how many. Write the number.

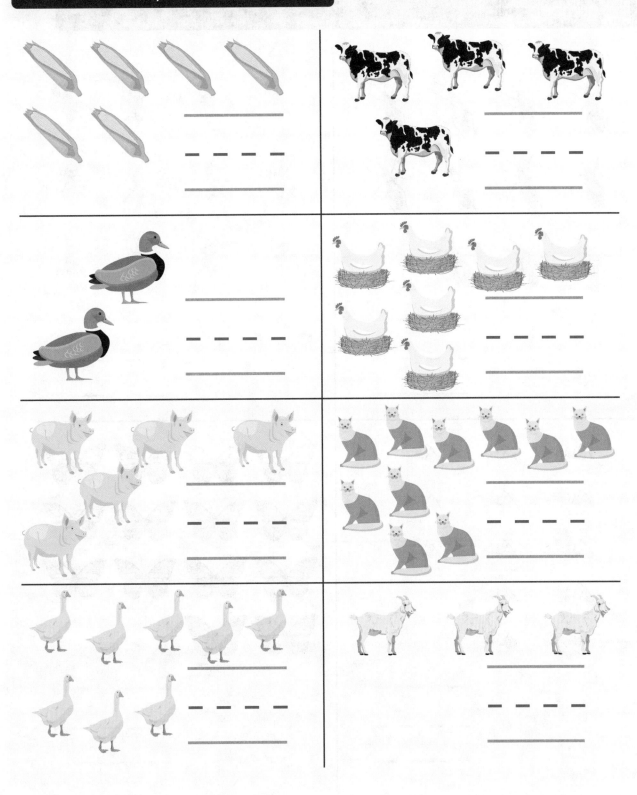

Lesson 1.20 Counting 11 through 14

Count the objects in each group out loud. Trace the number. Write the number.

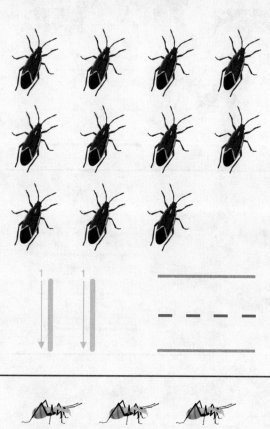

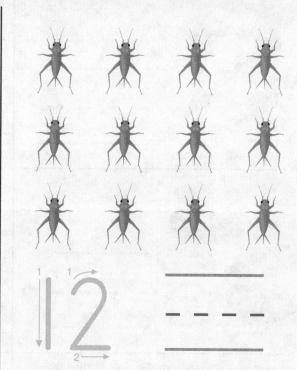

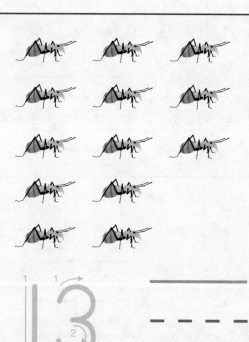

Lesson 1.21 Counting 15 through 18

Count the objects in each group out loud. Trace the number. Write the number.

15   - - - - -
      _ _ _ _ _

16   - - - - -
      _ _ _ _ _

17   - - - - -
      _ _ _ _ _

18   - - - - -
      _ _ _ _ _

Name _____

Lesson 1.22 Counting 19 through 22

Count the objects in each group out loud. Trace the number. Write the number.

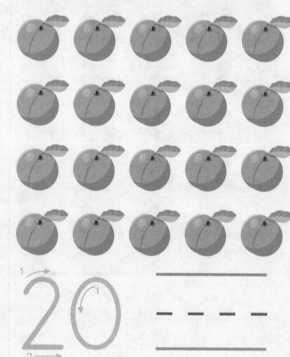

Lesson 1.23 Counting On: 0 through 20

Cut out the counters. For each ten frame, pick up a handful of counters. Put them in the box. Count. Write how many.

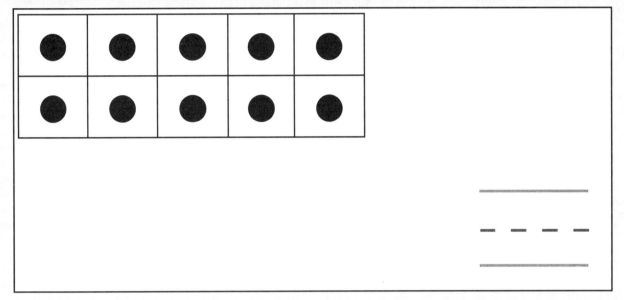

_ _ _ _ _ _ _

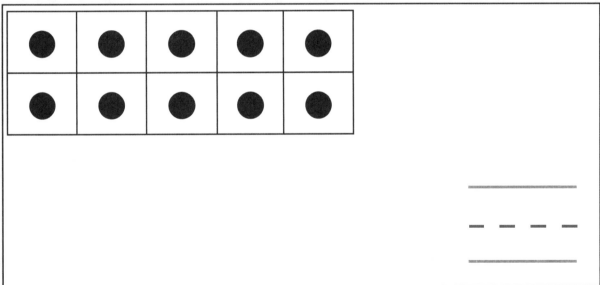

_ _ _ _ _ _ _

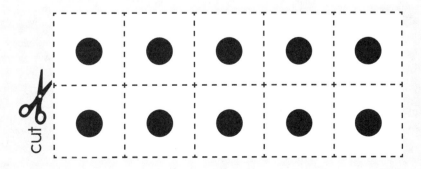

cut

Page intentionally left blank.

Name _____

Lesson 1.23 Counting On: 0 through 20

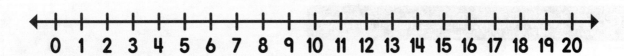

0 1 2 3 4 5 6 7 8 9 10 11 12 13 14 15 16 17 18 19 20

Use the number line to help you write the missing numbers.

3	

15	

12	

6	

10		12

4		6

18		20

7		9

	8

	2

	14

	17

Use the number line to count by 2s to 20. Write the numbers you land on.

2, _____, _____, _____, _____,

_____, _____, _____, _____, 20

Lesson 1.24 Counting and Writing 11 through 15

Count how many. Trace the number.

Lesson 1.25 Counting and Writing 16 through 20

Count how many. Trace the number.

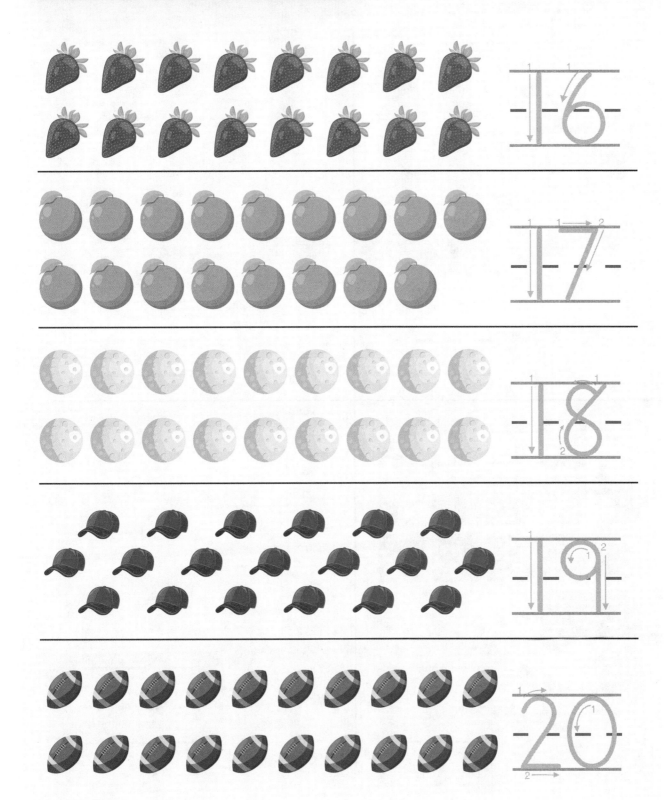

Lesson 1.26 Counting and Writing 0 through 20

Count how many. Write the number.

_____
_ _ _ _
_____

_____
_ _ _ _
_____

_____
_ _ _ _
_____

_____
_ _ _ _
_____

Lesson 1.26 Counting and Writing 0 through 20

Count how many. Write the number.

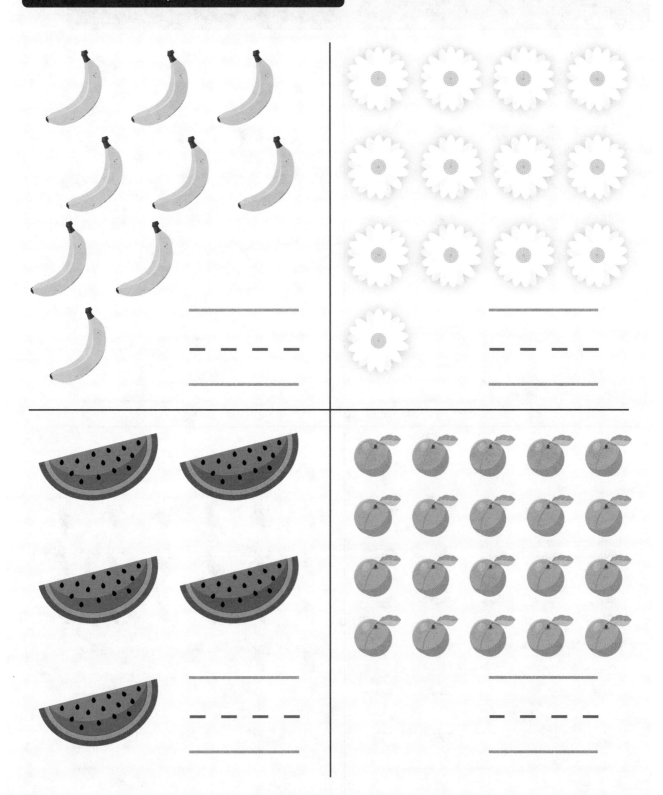

Name _____

Lesson 1.27 Counting 23 through 26

Count the objects in each group out loud. Trace the number. Write the number.

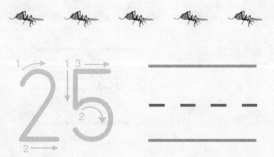

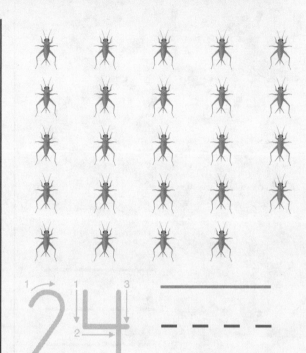

Spectrum Math **Kindergarten**

Name _____

Lesson 1.28 Counting 27 through 30

Count the objects in each group out loud. Trace the number. Write the number.

27 _ _ _ _ _

28 _ _ _ _ _

29 _ _ _ _ _

30 _ _ _ _ _

Lesson 1.29 Reading the Calendar

Trace and say the name of the month. Say the names of the days of the week. Trace and write the numbers to complete the calendar.

JULY

SUNDAY	MONDAY	TUESDAY	WEDNESDAY	THURSDAY	FRIDAY	SATURDAY
				1	2	3
		6	7			10
11		14		16		
	19				23	
25						31

Lesson 1.30 Counting to 100

Count the number of objects out loud by ones and by tens. Trace the number. Write the number.

Name _____

Lesson 1.30 Counting to 100

Fill in the missing numbers.

1		3	4	5		7	8	9	
11	12		14		16	17	18	19	20
21	22	23		25	26	27	28		30
31		33	34	35	36		38	39	40
41	42	43	44	45	46	47		49	50
	52	53	54		56	57	58	59	60
61	62	63	64	65			68	69	70
71	72		74	75	76	77		79	80
	82	83		85	86	87	88	89	
91	92	93	94	95	96	97	98		100

Lesson 1.30 Counting to 100

Use the number chart on page 46 to practice counting.

Count out loud from 1 to 100.

Count by tens from 10 to 100.

Start at 20. Count to 100.

Start at 50. Count to 100.

Use the number chart on page 46 to count on.

80, _____, _____, _____

73, _____, _____, _____

97, _____, _____, _____

Use the number chart to count by 5s. Put your finger on each number you land on. Get all the way to 100!

Review Chapter 1

Circle the objects in the group to match the given number.

This ten frame shows 4. Draw dots to show 9.

This ten frame shows 0. Draw dots to show 5.

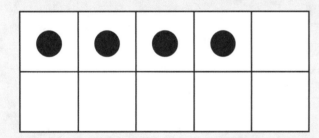

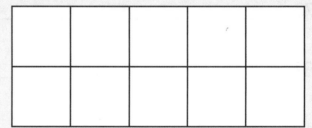

Count how many. Write the number.

_____

- - - - -
_____

_____

- - - - -
_____

Review Chapter 1

Circle the number.

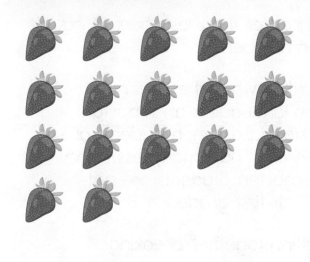 

| 16 | 17 | 18 | 22 | 23 | 24 |

Write the missing numbers.

| 9 | |

| 15 | |

| 12 | | 14 |

| 18 | | 20 |

| | 8 |

| | 15 |

Helpful Definitions ••••••••••••••••••••••••••••••••••••••

comparing numbers: using the words *greater than*, *less than*, or *equal to* to describe the relationship between numbers

Students will take their counting skills further when they learn to compare numbers. Gaining comparison language is an important kindergarten goal. It will support later standards when students are expected to answer "how many more?" and "how many less?" The language is the important skill for kindergarten. Students are not expected to use the symbols >, <, or = until first grade.

composing/decomposing numbers: putting together/breaking numbers apart in different ways

Composing and decomposing numbers is one way for your student to begin to understand addition and subtraction. Help your student practice by asking them to show the same number by holding up a different number of fingers on each hand.

number bond: a visual representation of the relationship between a pair of numbers and the sum of those numbers; this is a helpful way to show the part-part whole relationship of the numbers

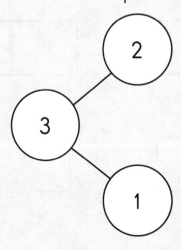

Skills Checklist

☐ Compare the number of objects in one group to another group using *greater than*, *less than*, or *equal to*

☐ Compare two numerals between 1 and 10 using *greater than*, *less than*, or *equal to*

☐ Decompose numbers through 10

☐ Compose and decompose numbers from 11 to 19 into a ten and some ones

Tools and Tips

linking cubes: individual cubes that can connect

These cubes can be used to help with visualization for various early math concepts such as sorting, counting, addition, and subtraction. In this book there is a visual representation of the tool.

Lesson 2.1 Comparing Numbers 0 through 5

You can use the words *greater than* or *less than* to compare groups.

3 is **greater than** 2.   2 is **less than** 3.

Count the objects. Circle the group that is greater.

Count the objects. Circle the group that is less.

Lesson 2.1 Comparing Numbers 0 through 5

Circle the number that is greater.

5   3 | 2   4

3   1 | 1   2

Circle the number that is less.

5   1 | 3   4

4   1 | 5   2

Lesson 2.2 Comparing Numbers 6 through 9

Count the objects. Circle the group that is greater.

Count the objects. Circle the group that is less.

Lesson 2.2 Comparing Numbers 6 through 9

Circle the number that is greater.

6   8   6   9

9   7   7   8

Circle the number that is less.

7   6   9   6

6   8   7   8

Lesson 2.3 Comparing Numbers 0 through 9

Count the objects in each set. Look at the set that has more. Draw Xs on objects in that set to make both sets the same, or equal.

You can use the symbols > (greater than), < (less than), and = (equal to) to compare numbers. Use the symbols to compare the numbers.

1 6   3 ◯ 2   9 7

Lesson 2.4 Decomposing Numbers through 10

You can make 4 in different ways.

    2 and 2   or   3 and 1

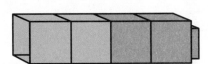
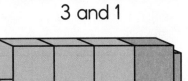

Use two colors to color the cubes in different ways. Write the numbers.

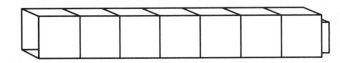

_____ and _____ make _____.

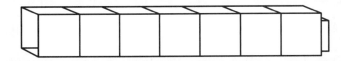

_____ and _____ make _____.

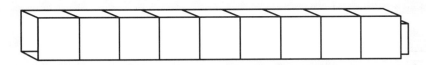

_____ and _____ make _____.

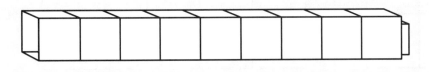

_____ and _____ make _____.

Lesson 2.5 Composing Numbers 11 through 19

Draw dots to show the number sentences.

10 and 2 is 12.

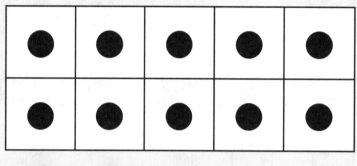

10 and 5 is 15.

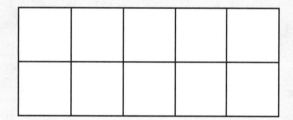

10 and 8 is 18.

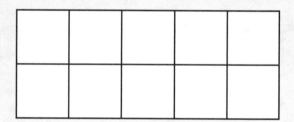

10 and 1 is 11.

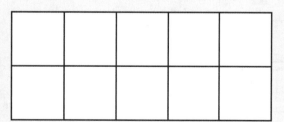

10 and 7 is 17.

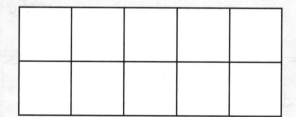

Lesson 2.6 Decomposing Numbers 11 through 19

Write the number sentence shown in the ten frame.

16 is 10 and 6.

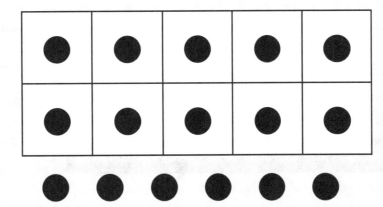

14 is _____ and _____.

19 is _____ and _____.

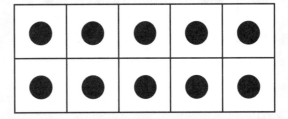

12 is _____ and _____.

13 is _____ and _____.

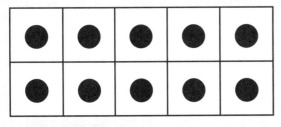

Lesson 2.7 Composing and Decomposing Numbers 11 through 19

Draw dots to show the number sentences.

10 and 3 is 13.

10 and 9 is 19.

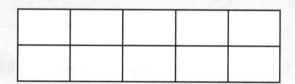

Write the number sentence shown in the ten frame.

17 is _____ and _____.

15 is _____ and _____.

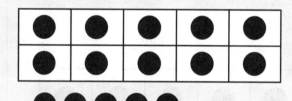

Write the missing number in the number bond.

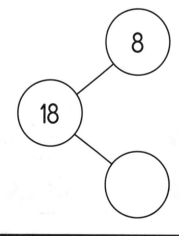

Name _____

Lesson 2.7 Composing and Decomposing Numbers 11 through 19

Use the ten frame and counters to show the numbers. Then, say the number sentence for each number. Practice showing more numbers and saying their number sentences.

12   **18**   **14**

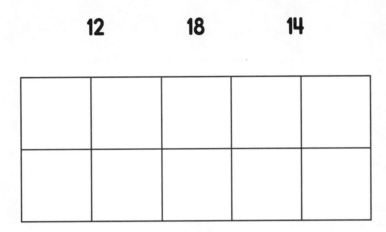

cut ✂

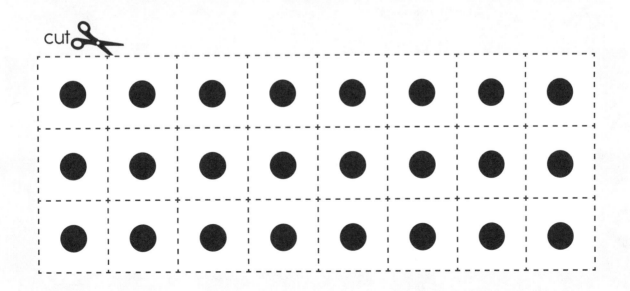

Spectrum Math **Kindergarten**

61

Page intentionally left blank.

Review Chapter 2

Count the objects. Circle the group that is greater.

Count the objects. Circle the group that is less.

Circle the number that is greater.

4   5 | 8   2

Circle the number that is less.

6   3 | 4   9

Name _____

Review Chapter 2

Use two colors to show the number 8 in two ways.

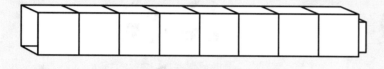

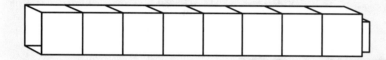

Write the number sentence shown in the ten frame.

15 is _____ and _____.

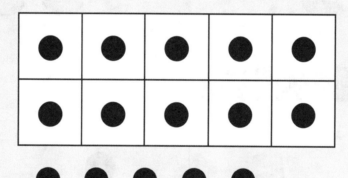

18 is _____ and _____.

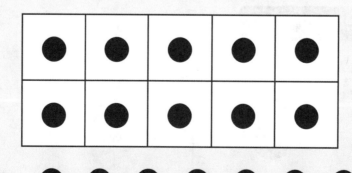

Learning Checkpoint Chapters 1–2

Count the objects. Circle the number.

6   9   8

12   18   16

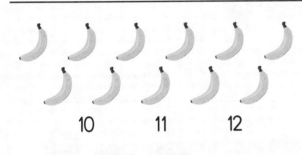

10   11   12

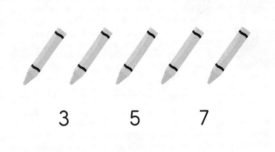

3   5   7

Color the objects to make the number shown.

8

12

3

18

Learning Checkpoint Chapters 1–2

Count how many. Write the number.

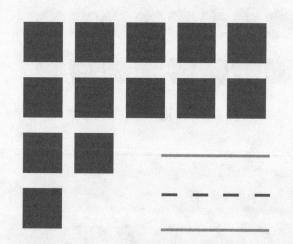

_____

- - - - - - - - -

_____

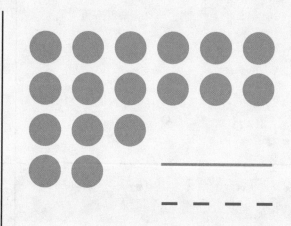

_____

- - - - - - - - -

_____

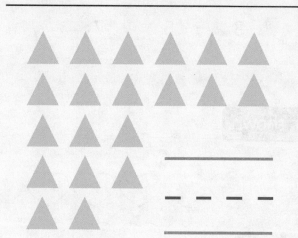

_____

- - - - - - - - -

_____

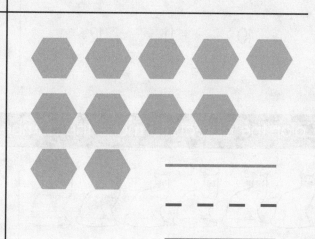

_____

- - - - - - - - -

_____

This ten frame shows 9. Draw a dot to show 10.

Learning Checkpoint Chapters 1–2

Write the missing number.

| 19 | |

| 3 | | 5 |

| | 17 |

Color the numbers you say when you count by tens to 100.

1	2	3	4	5	6	7	8	9	10
11	12	13	14	15	16	17	18	19	20
21	22	23	24	25	26	27	28	29	30
31	32	33	34	35	36	37	38	39	40
41	42	43	44	45	46	47	48	49	50
51	52	53	54	55	56	57	58	59	60
61	62	63	64	65	66	67	68	69	70
71	72	73	74	75	76	77	78	79	80
81	82	83	84	85	86	87	88	89	90
91	92	93	94	95	96	97	98	99	100

Name _____

Learning Checkpoint Chapters 1–2

Count the objects in the first set. Use red to color the set that is greater. Use yellow to color the set that is less. If there is a set that is the same, or equal, color it blue.

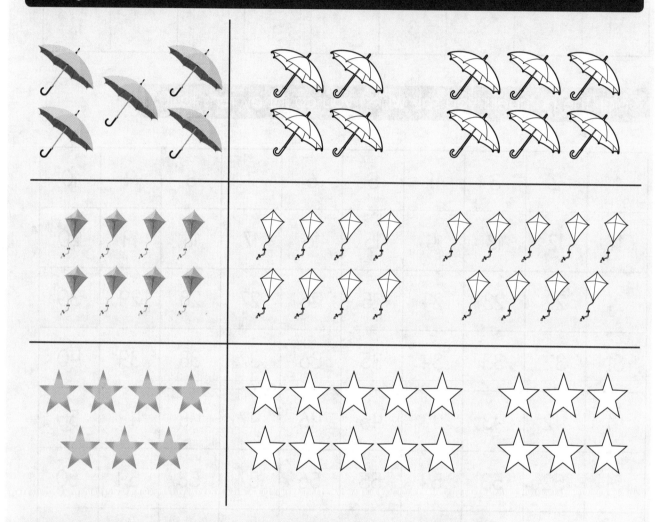

Use two colors to show the number 5 in different ways. Write the numbers.

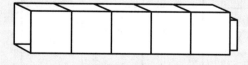
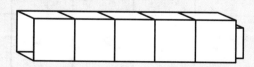

_____ and _____ make _____.   _____ and _____ make _____.

Name _____

Learning Checkpoint Chapters 1–2

Use the ten frame to show the number sentence.

10 and 4 is 14.

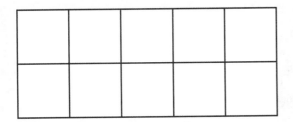

10 and 9 is 19.

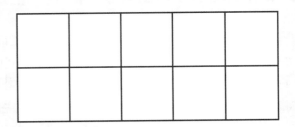

Write the number sentence shown in the ten frame.

11 is _____ and _____.

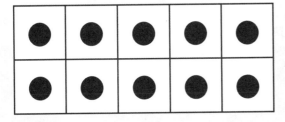

17 is _____ and _____.

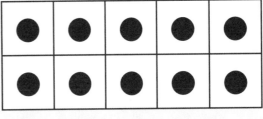

Chapter 3: Addition and Subtraction

Helpful Definitions

math fluency: the ability to quickly recall equations such as addition and subtraction facts

While it is important for your student to understand how addition and subtraction work, it is also important for them to learn to solve problems quickly and correctly in their head. When your student is able to do this, they have developed fluency with this skill.

word problem: a math problem expressed with words, usually describing a real-life scenario where the math concept could occur

Skills Checklist

☐ Add and subtract within 10

☐ Fluently add and subtract within 5

☐ Solve addition and subtraction word problems

☐ Find the number that makes 10 when added to any number 1–9

Making 10

Learning what numbers add up to 10 is an important math strategy that your student will revisit in first grade. This strategy allows for the quick addition of numbers in order to create easily solvable equations. Practice will sharpen mental math skills and assist with math fluency.

Clue Words

In the future, your student will need to identify what math operation needs to be done to solve a word problem. To help your student prepare for this, point out the clue words that make a word problem either addition or subtraction:

Addition	Subtraction
in all	fewer
sum	left
total	take away
altogether	minus
plus	difference
add	remain

If your student is struggling with this introduction to word problems, here are some ways you can help:
- Read the problem out loud.
- Circle all the numbers in the problem.
- Underline what you're being asked to find.
- Draw a picture of the problem.
- Use objects such as toys to act out the problem.

Lesson 3.1 Adding More (Addition)

There are 2 kittens on the rug. There is 1 kitten off the rug. Count the total number of kittens. Trace the number that shows how many kittens in all.

There are 3 frogs on one lily pad and 1 frog on another lily pad. Count the number of frogs altogether. Trace the number that shows the number of frogs.

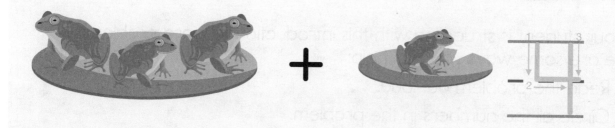

Name _____

Lesson 3.1 Adding More (Addition)

There are 2 red kites and 2 blue kites in the sky. How many kites are there in all?

There are 2 apples in a bowl. There are 3 oranges in a bowl. How much fruit is there in all?

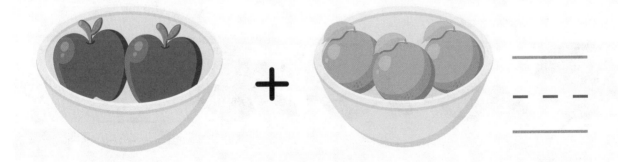

Lesson 3.2 Taking Away (Subtraction)

There are 3 fish in a pond. Then, 1 fish swims away. Count the number of fish that are left. Trace the number that shows how many fish are left.

There are 4 baseball caps hanging on a hat rack. Then, 1 cap is taken away. Count the number of caps that are left. Trace the number that shows how many caps are left.

Lesson 3.2 Taking Away (Subtraction)

There are 2 butterflies on a flower. Then, 1 flies away. How many are left?

There are 5 tomatoes on a vine. Then, 3 are picked. How many are left on the vine?

Lesson 3.3 Adding through 3

Count the total number of objects in each section. Write the number.

$$\begin{array}{r} 1 \\ +\ 1 \\ \hline \end{array}$$

$$\begin{array}{r} 2 \\ +\ 1 \\ \hline \end{array}$$

$$\begin{array}{r} 3 \\ +\ 0 \\ \hline \end{array}$$

$$\begin{array}{r} 1 \\ +\ 2 \\ \hline \end{array}$$

$$\begin{array}{r} 0 \\ +\ 2 \\ \hline \end{array}$$

Lesson 3.4 Subtracting through 3

Count the number of objects left after the crossed-out objects are removed. Write the number of remaining objects.

$$\begin{array}{r} 3 \\ -1 \\ \hline \end{array}$$

$$\begin{array}{r} 1 \\ -1 \\ \hline \end{array}$$

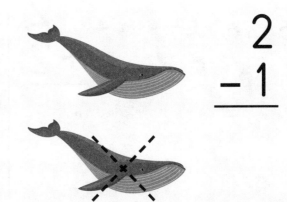

$$\begin{array}{r} 2 \\ -1 \\ \hline \end{array}$$

$$\begin{array}{r} 3 \\ -2 \\ \hline \end{array}$$

$$\begin{array}{r} 3 \\ -0 \\ \hline \end{array}$$

Lesson 3.5 Adding to 4 and 5

Count the total number of objects in each section. Write the number.

$$\begin{array}{r} 3 \\ +2 \\ \hline \end{array}$$

$$\begin{array}{r} 2 \\ +2 \\ \hline \end{array}$$

$$\begin{array}{r} 3 \\ +1 \\ \hline \end{array}$$

$$\begin{array}{r} 1 \\ +4 \\ \hline \end{array}$$

$$\begin{array}{r} 2 \\ +3 \\ \hline \end{array}$$

Lesson 3.6 Subtracting from 4 and 5

Count the number of objects left after the crossed-out objects are removed. Write the number of remaining objects.

$$\begin{array}{r} 5 \\ -3 \\ \hline \end{array}$$

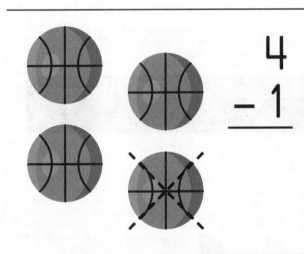

$$\begin{array}{r} 4 \\ -1 \\ \hline \end{array}$$

$$\begin{array}{r} 5 \\ -2 \\ \hline \end{array}$$

$$\begin{array}{r} 5 \\ -4 \\ \hline \end{array}$$

$$\begin{array}{r} 4 \\ -2 \\ \hline \end{array}$$

Lesson 3.7 Adding through 5

There is 1 tree in the park. Then, 2 more trees grow. How many total trees are there in the park now?

_____ trees

There are 4 bats in a cave. There is 1 bat outside the cave. How many bats are there in all?

_____ bats

Lesson 3.8 Subtracting within 5

There are 5 peaches on the tree. Then, 2 of the peaches get picked. How many peaches are left?

_____ peaches

There are 4 bats in a cave. Then, 3 bats fly out of the cave. How many bats are left?

_____ bat

Lesson 3.9 Adding to 6 and 7

Count the total number of objects in each section. Write the number.

$$\begin{array}{r} 3 \\ +\ 4 \\ \hline \end{array}$$

$$\begin{array}{r} 2 \\ +\ 5 \\ \hline \end{array}$$

$$\begin{array}{r} 4 \\ +\ 2 \\ \hline \end{array}$$

$$\begin{array}{r} 3 \\ +\ 3 \\ \hline \end{array}$$

$$\begin{array}{r} 4 \\ +\ 3 \\ \hline \end{array}$$

Name _____

Lesson 3.10 Subtracting from 6 and 7

Count the number of objects left after the crossed-out objects are removed. Write the number of remaining objects.

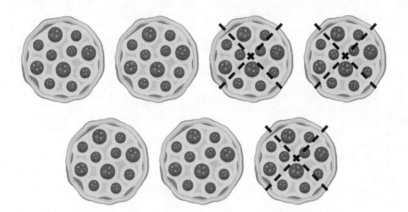

$$\begin{array}{r} 7 \\ -3 \\ \hline \end{array}$$

$$\begin{array}{r} 6 \\ -4 \\ \hline \end{array}$$

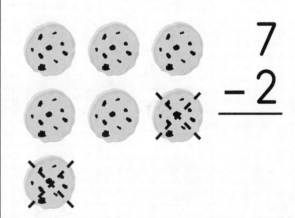

$$\begin{array}{r} 7 \\ -2 \\ \hline \end{array}$$

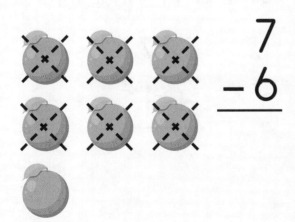

$$\begin{array}{r} 7 \\ -6 \\ \hline \end{array}$$

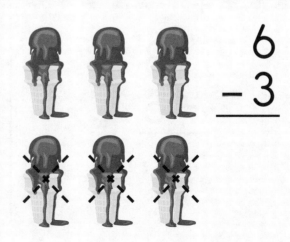

$$\begin{array}{r} 6 \\ -3 \\ \hline \end{array}$$

Lesson 3.11 Adding to 8 and 9

Count the total number of objects in each section. Write the number.

$$\begin{array}{r} 5 \\ +3 \\ \hline \end{array}$$

$$\begin{array}{r} 4 \\ +5 \\ \hline \end{array}$$

$$\begin{array}{r} 6 \\ +2 \\ \hline \end{array}$$

$$\begin{array}{r} 3 \\ +6 \\ \hline \end{array}$$

$$\begin{array}{r} 7 \\ +1 \\ \hline \end{array}$$

Spectrum Math **Kindergarten**

Lesson 3.12 Subtracting from 8 and 9

Count the number of objects left after the crossed-out objects are removed. Write the number of remaining objects.

$$\begin{array}{r} 9 \\ -2 \\ \hline \end{array}$$

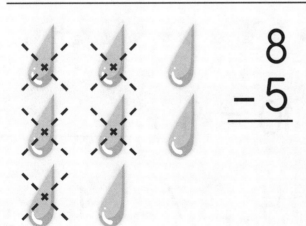

$$\begin{array}{r} 8 \\ -3 \\ \hline \end{array}$$

$$\begin{array}{r} 9 \\ -6 \\ \hline \end{array}$$

$$\begin{array}{r} 8 \\ -5 \\ \hline \end{array}$$

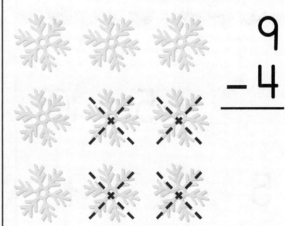

$$\begin{array}{r} 9 \\ -4 \\ \hline \end{array}$$

Lesson 3.13 Making 10

Count the total number of objects in each set. Circle the number that makes 10.

6 + _____ = 10   1   4   2

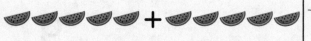	(bees images) + (bees)
_____ + 3 = 10	10 = 8 + _____
5 7 4	3 5 2

(watermelon images) + (watermelon)	(leaf images) + (leaf)
_____ + 5 = 10	10 = 9 + _____
5 8 9	4 7 1

Lesson 3.13 Making 10

Draw the missing dots. Write the number you drew to make 10.

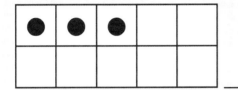

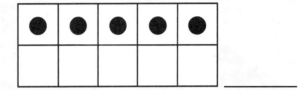

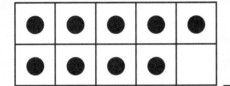

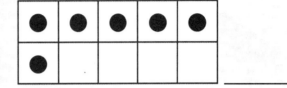

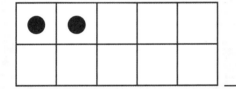

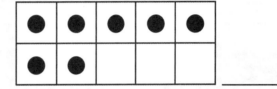

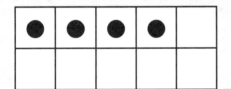

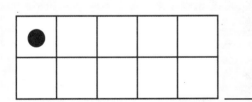

Ivy has 6 strawberries in her lunch. How many more does she need to make 10? _____

Lesson 3.14 Subtracting from 10

Count the number of objects left. Write the number of remaining objects.

$$\begin{array}{r} 10 \\ -4 \\ \hline \end{array}$$

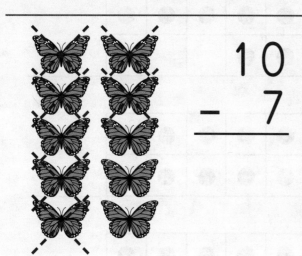

$$\begin{array}{r} 10 \\ -7 \\ \hline \end{array}$$

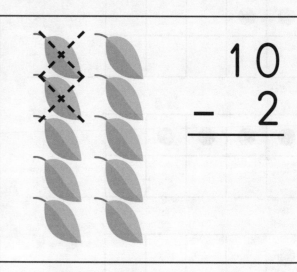

$$\begin{array}{r} 10 \\ -2 \\ \hline \end{array}$$

$$\begin{array}{r} 10 \\ -5 \\ \hline \end{array}$$

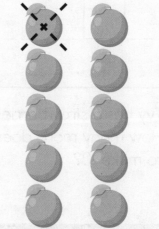

$$\begin{array}{r} 10 \\ -1 \\ \hline \end{array}$$

Lesson 3.15 Adding Numbers

Add.

$$\begin{array}{r} 3 \\ +3 \\ \hline \end{array}$$

$$\begin{array}{r} 4 \\ +2 \\ \hline \end{array}$$

$$\begin{array}{r} 8 \\ +2 \\ \hline \end{array}$$

$$\begin{array}{r} 5 \\ +3 \\ \hline \end{array}$$

$$\begin{array}{r} 3 \\ +6 \\ \hline \end{array}$$

$$\begin{array}{r} 7 \\ +1 \\ \hline \end{array}$$

Lesson 3.15 Adding Numbers

Add.

$$
\begin{array}{r}
3 \\
+2 \\
\hline
\end{array}
\qquad
\begin{array}{r}
3 \\
+1 \\
\hline
\end{array}
$$

$$
\begin{array}{r}
0 \\
+5 \\
\hline
\end{array}
\qquad
\begin{array}{r}
1 \\
+1 \\
\hline
\end{array}
$$

$$
\begin{array}{r}
2 \\
+2 \\
\hline
\end{array}
\qquad
\begin{array}{r}
4 \\
+1 \\
\hline
\end{array}
$$

Lesson 3.15 Adding Numbers

Cut out the apples. Use them to solve the problems.

There are 3 red apples and 4 green apples. How many apples are there in all?

_____ apples

There are 5 red apples and 1 green apple. How many apples are there in all?

_____ apples

There are 2 red apples and 3 green apples. How many apples are there in all?

_____ apples

There are 2 red apples and 5 green apples. How many apples are there in all?

_____ apples

cut ✂

Page intentionally left blank.

Name _____

Lesson 3.15 Adding Numbers

Write a number sentence to help you solve each problem.

Amir saw 5 birds. Jada saw 1 bird. How many birds did they see in all?

_____ + _____ = _____ birds

_____

Kiara has 3 fish. Deja has 4 fish. How many fish do they have in all?

_____ + _____ = _____ fish

_____

Mei kicked 2 balls. Finn kicked 6 balls. How many balls did they kick in all?

_____ + _____ = _____ balls

_____

Hiro drew 6 pictures. Eve drew 3 pictures. How many pictures did they draw in all?

_____ + _____ = _____ pictures

Name _____

Lesson 3.16 Subtracting Numbers

Subtract.

$$\begin{array}{r} 8 \\ -\ 3 \\ \hline \end{array}$$

$$\begin{array}{r} 9 \\ -\ 9 \\ \hline \end{array}$$

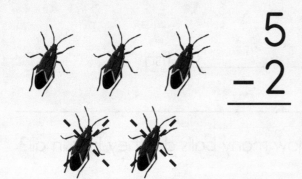
$$\begin{array}{r} 5 \\ -\ 2 \\ \hline \end{array}$$

$$\begin{array}{r} 7 \\ -\ 5 \\ \hline \end{array}$$

$$\begin{array}{r} 6 \\ -\ 3 \\ \hline \end{array}$$

$$\begin{array}{r} 10 \\ -\ 5 \\ \hline \end{array}$$

94

Spectrum Math **Kindergarten**

Lesson 3.16 Subtracting Numbers

Subtract.

$$\begin{array}{r} 3 \\ -2 \\ \hline \end{array}$$

$$\begin{array}{r} 2 \\ -1 \\ \hline \end{array}$$

$$\begin{array}{r} 1 \\ -1 \\ \hline \end{array}$$

$$\begin{array}{r} 4 \\ -2 \\ \hline \end{array}$$

$$\begin{array}{r} 3 \\ -0 \\ \hline \end{array}$$

$$\begin{array}{r} 4 \\ -3 \\ \hline \end{array}$$

Lesson 3.16 Subtracting Numbers

Write a number sentence to help you solve each problem.

Gia has 6 cookies. She eats 1 cookie. How many cookies does Gia have left?

_____ − _____ = _____ cookies

_____

Hasan has 7 flowers. He gives 6 flowers to his grandma. How many flowers does Hasan have left?

_____ − _____ = _____ flowers

_____

Nadia has 8 coins. She loses 4 coins. How many coins does Nadia have left?

_____ − _____ = _____ coins

_____

Ryder has 9 cherries. He eats 7 cherries. How many cherries does Ryder have left?

_____ − _____ = _____ cherries

Lesson 3.16 Subtracting Numbers

Cut out the balloons. Use them to solve the problems.

You have 6 balloons. You pop 3 balloons. How many balloons do you have left?

_____ balloons

You have 8 balloons. You pop 2 balloons. How many balloons do you have left?

_____ balloons

You have 5 balloons. You pop 3 balloons. How many balloons do you have left?

_____ balloons

You have 7 balloons. You pop 1 balloon. How many balloons do you have left?

_____ balloons

cut

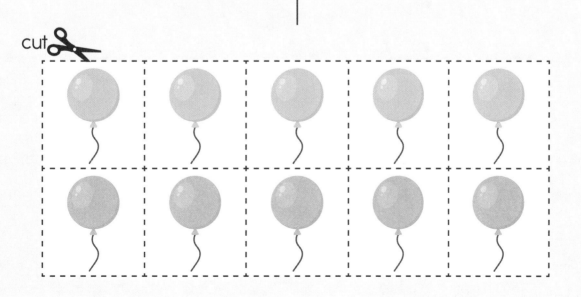

Page intentionally left blank.

Name _____

Review Chapter 3

Add.

$$\begin{array}{r} 4 \\ +4 \\ \hline \end{array} \qquad \begin{array}{r} 5 \\ +2 \\ \hline \end{array}$$

Subtract.

$$\begin{array}{r} 6 \\ -3 \\ \hline \end{array} \qquad \begin{array}{r} 9 \\ -1 \\ \hline \end{array}$$

Name _____

Review Chapter 3

Draw the missing dots. Write the number you drew to make 10.

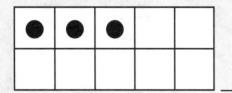

●	●	●		

_____

●	●	●	●	●

_____

Add.

There are 2 dogs at the dog park. Then, 1 more dog comes to the dog park. How many total dogs are at the dog park?

+ ☐ = _____ dogs

Subtract.

There are 5 ice-cream cones. Then, 2 ice-cream cones get eaten. How many ice-cream cones are left?

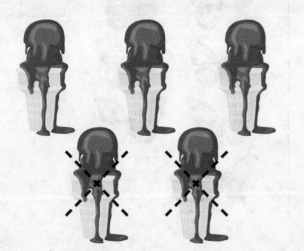

_____ ice-cream cones

Spectrum Math **Kindergarten**

Helpful Definitions ••••••••••••••••••••••••••••••••••••

measurable attributes: the aspects of an object that can be measured, such as length, weight, and size

The giraffe is
tall and **heavy**.

standard unit: an accepted unit of measurement, such as an inch or a centimeter

non-standard unit: any item used for measurement that is not a standard unit

A non-standard unit could be a paperclip, penny, crayon, or any object used to measure that isn't a standard unit. Measuring with non-standard units helps your student understand the concept of measurement before they are introduced to standard units.

Skills Checklist ••••••••••••••••••••••••••••••••••••

☐ Describe the measurable attributes of an object

☐ Compare the measurable attributes of two objects

☐ Sort objects into given categories

Lesson 4.1 Measurable Attributes

You can use words such as *light*, *heavy*, *short*, and *tall* to describe an object.

The flower is **short** and **light**.

> Circle the word that best describes each object.

light   heavy

light   heavy

short   tall

short   tall

Lesson 4.1 Measurable Attributes

Complete each sentence. Draw a picture.

I am lighter than _____

_____ .

I am heavier than _____

_____ .

I am shorter than _____

_____ .

I am taller than _____

_____ .

Lesson 4.2 Longer and Shorter

Color the shorter object in each row green. Color the longer object blue. The first one has been done for you.

Name _____

Lesson 4.3 Describing an Object

Circle the word that describes how each object compares to the paperclip.

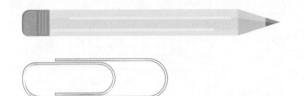

longer   shorter

longer   shorter

longer   shorter

0   Inches   1   2   3

longer   shorter

The last problem on this page shows a ruler next to the paperclip. The numbers on the ruler measure inches. How many inches long is the paperclip? _____

Name _____

Lesson 4.4 Taller and Shorter

Circle the taller object in each section. Draw an X on the shorter object.

 Draw an animal that is taller than the cat. Number the cat, mouse, and your drawing from shortest (1) to tallest (3).

Spectrum Math **Kindergarten**

Name _____

Lesson 4.5 Describing an Object

Circle the word that describes how each object compares to the tree.

taller   shorter

taller   shorter

taller   shorter

taller   shorter

Spectrum Math **Kindergarten**

Lesson 4.6 Heavier and Lighter

Circle the heavier object in each section. Draw an X on the lighter object.

Name _____

Lesson 4.7 Describing an Object

Circle the word that describes how each object compares to the bike.

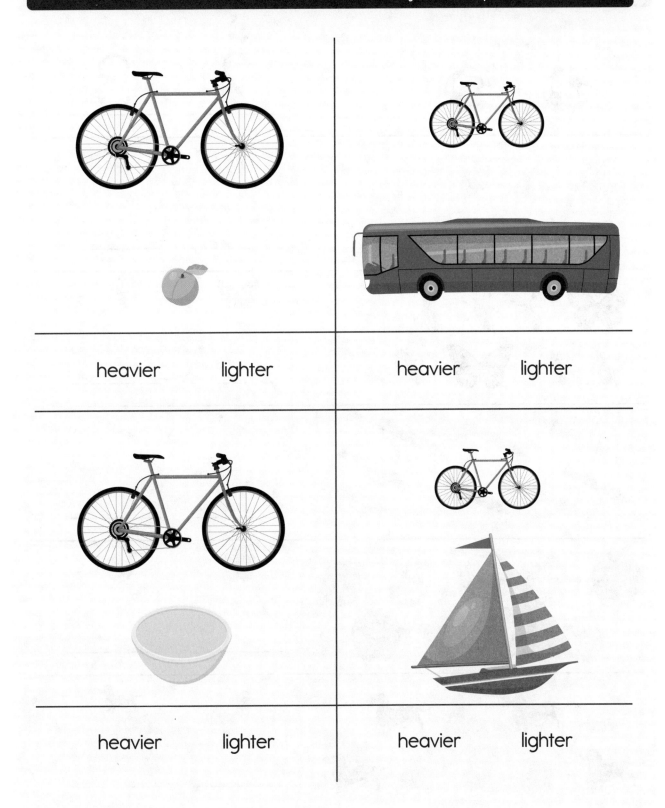

| heavier   lighter | heavier   lighter |
| heavier   lighter | heavier   lighter |

Name _____

Lesson 4.8 Sorting and Classifying Objects

How many? Write the number. The first one has been done for you.

	⚽	⚾
	2	3

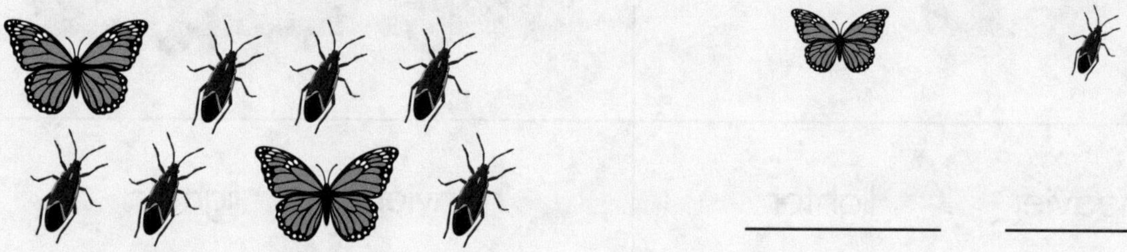

Leaves: _____ _____

Bugs: _____ _____

Crayons: _____ _____

Apples: _____ _____

Cats and dogs: _____ _____

Name _____

Lesson 4.8 Sorting and Classifying Objects

How many? Write the number.

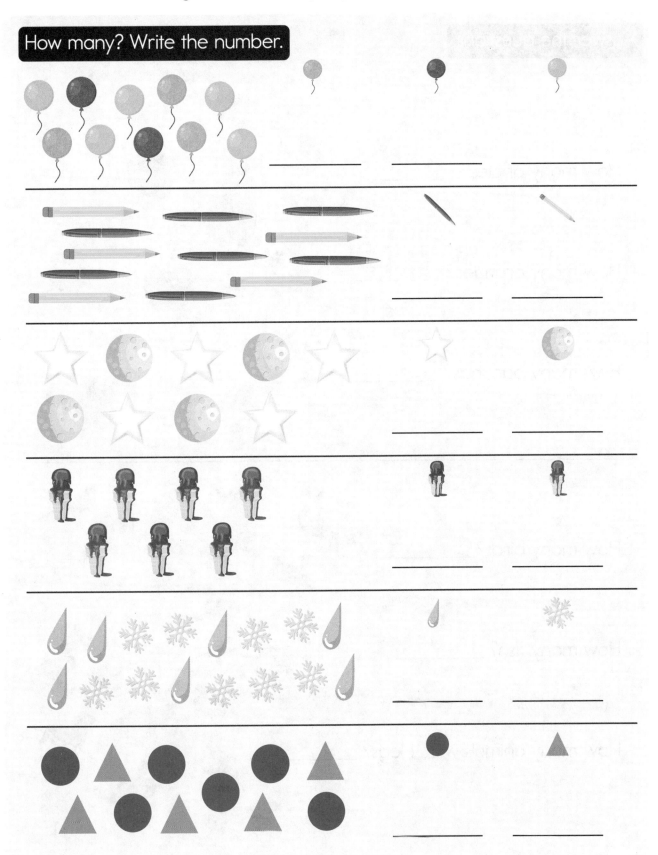

_____   _____   _____

_____   _____

_____   _____

_____   _____

_____   _____

_____   _____

Name _____

Lesson 4.8 Sorting and Classifying Objects

Answer the questions.

How many apples? _____

How many oranges? _____

How many bananas? _____

_____

How many birds? _____

How many fish? _____

How many animals with 4 legs? _____

Name _____

Lesson 4.8 Sorting and Classifying Objects

Cut out the pictures. Sort and glue the pictures. Then, write how many.

square	triangle	circle

How many  ? _____   How many small shapes? _____

How many ▲ ? _____   How many large shapes? _____

How many ● ? _____

cut ✂

Page intentionally left blank.

Lesson 4.8 Sorting and Classifying Objects

Color the underwater animals blue. Color the land animals gray.

How many underwater animals? _____

How many land animals? _____

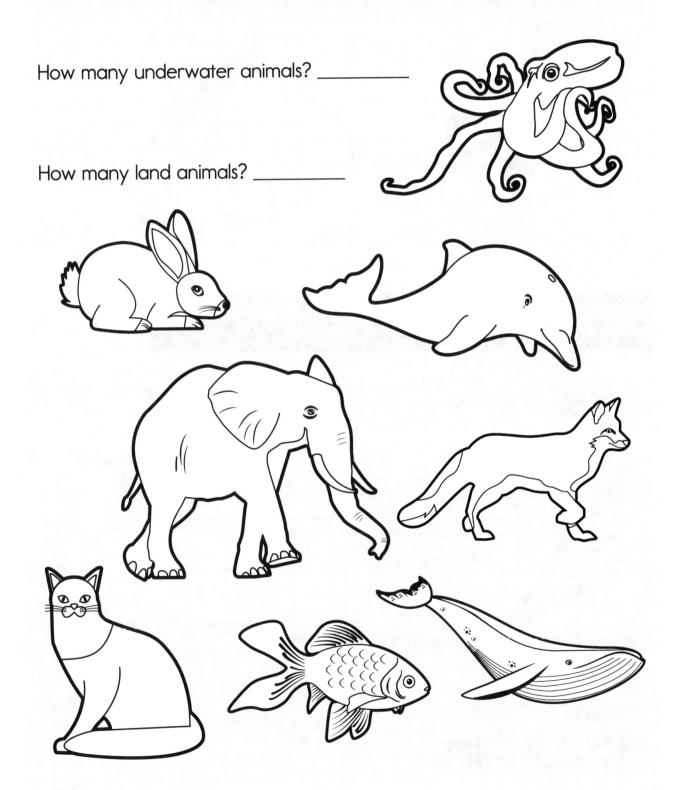

Review Chapter 4

Circle the word that best describes each object.

light   heavy

short   tall

Circle the word that describes how each object compares to the crayon.

longer   shorter

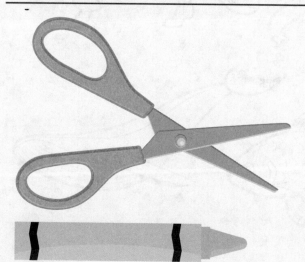

longer   shorter

Name _____

Review Chapter 4

Circle the word that describes how each object compares to the elephant.

lighter   heavier

shorter   taller

How many? Write the number.

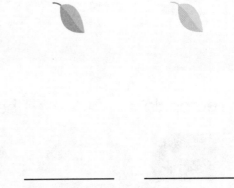

_____   _____

_____   _____

Chapter 5: Geometry

Helpful Definitions

two dimensional (2-D) shapes: shapes that are flat and have two dimensions, such as length and width

three dimensional (3-D) shapes: shapes that are solid and have three dimensions, such as length, width, and depth

For kindergarten, your student should know the shapes below.

square

circle

triangle

rectangle

hexagon

cube

cone

cylinder

sphere

Skills Checklist

☐ Identify shapes in your environment

☐ Use position words

☐ Know shape names and how to draw them

☐ Identify and compare 2-D vs 3-D shapes

☐ Combine shapes to form other shapes

Tools and Tips

Position Words

Position words help your student develop spatial awareness, an important early math skill. You can help your student by talking about where things are. Choose an item in the room. Give your student clues about whether it is above, below, or next to. Can your student find the item? Have your student give you clues, too.

Recognizing 3-D Shapes

Recognizing 3-D shapes is an important skill. You can help your student identify 3-D shapes in the real world (balls, cans of food, cereal boxes, etc.) and tell how they are different from 2-D shapes. Encourage your student to form solid shapes from modeling clay.

Combining Shapes

Stack and build with blocks to practice combining 3-D shapes. Or, stack and build with soup cans, food boxes, small balls, etc. Which shapes have flat surfaces and which do not? Ask your student to explain why some shapes stack easily and some do not.

Lesson 5.1 Flat Shapes (2-D)

square	rectangle	triangle	circle	hexagon

Color the shapes to match the shapes at the top of the page.

 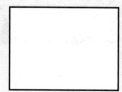 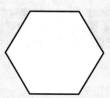

  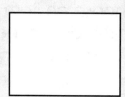

 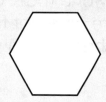

Lesson 5.2 Solid Shapes (3-D)

sphere	cone	cylinder	cube

Color the shapes to match the shapes at the top of the page.

Lesson 5.3 Identifying 2-D and 3-D Shapes

Circle all the 2-D shapes. Mark an X on all of the 3-D shapes.

Name _____

Lesson 5.3 Identifying 2-D and 3-D Shapes

Color the 2-D shapes red. Color the 3-D shapes blue.

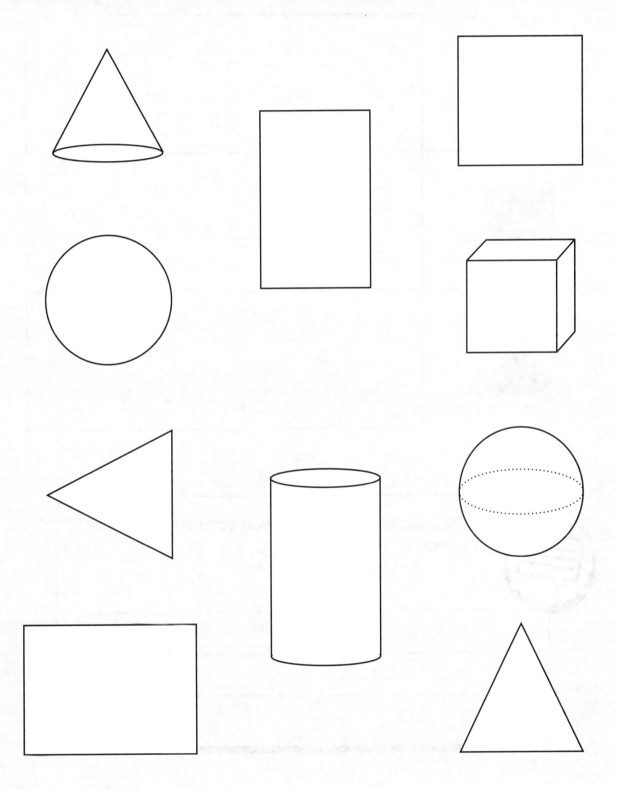

Name _____

Lesson 5.4 Comparing Shapes

Draw the flat faces of each shape.

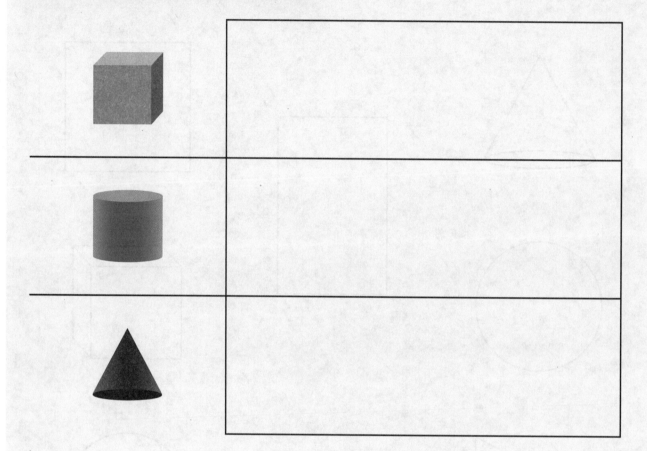

 Write a sentence that tells how a cone and a cylinder are alike.

_____

_____

_____

124

Lesson 5.4 Comparing Shapes

Compare the shapes. How are they similar? How are they different? The first one has been done for you.

Shapes	Similarities	Differences
	Both have straight sides Both have corners Both are 2-D	The square has 4 sides, and the triangle has 3

Name _____

Lesson 5.5 Position Words

Color the animals that are above the squirrel blue. Color the animals that are below the squirrel black. Color the animal next to the squirrel yellow. Finish coloring the scene.

 Draw an animal beside the tree.

Lesson 5.5 Position Words

Cut out the cars. Glue the red car in front of the blue car. Glue the green car behind the blue car.

cut ✂

Page intentionally left blank.

Name _____

Lesson 5.5 Position Words

Color the animals that are below the boat purple. Color the animals that are above the boat gray. Color the animal next to the boat brown. Finish coloring the scene.

Name _____

Lesson 5.6 Squares

Circle the square shapes.

Lesson 5.7 Rectangles

Circle the rectangular shapes.

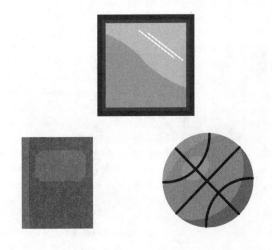

Name _____

Lesson 5.8 Triangles

Circle the triangular shapes.

Name _____

Lesson 5.9 Circles

Circle the circular shapes.

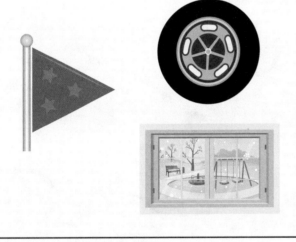

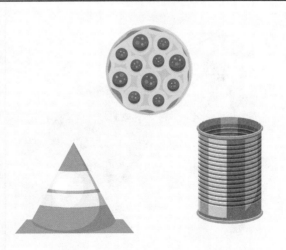

Lesson 5.10 Hexagons

Circle the hexagonal shapes.

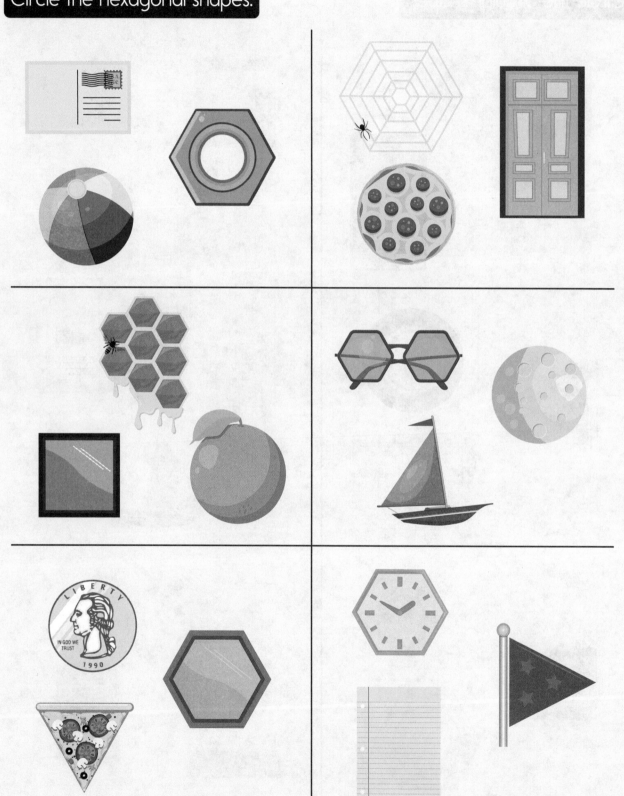

Lesson 5.11 Sorting Shapes

Color the circles red. Color the triangles blue. Color the squares green.
Color the rectangles yellow. Color the hexagons orange.

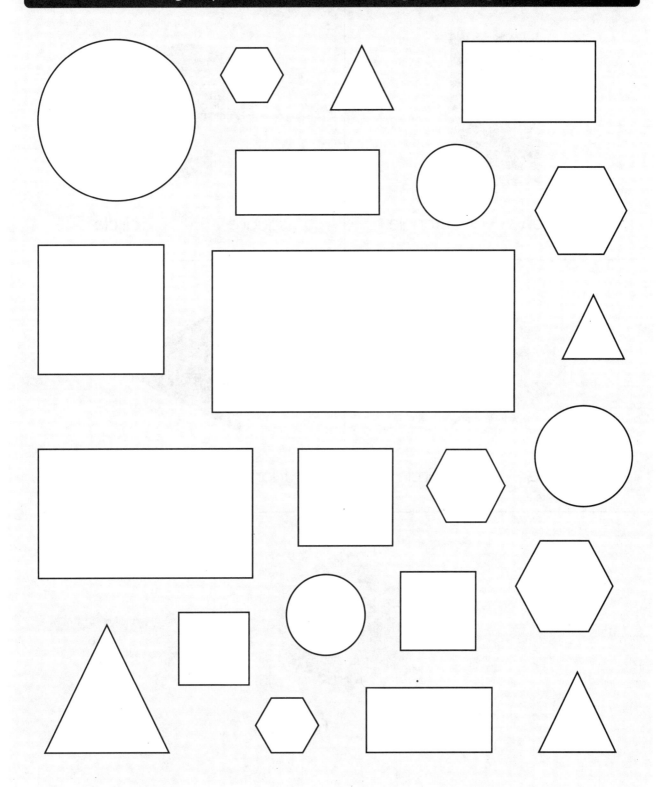

Lesson 5.12 Naming Shapes

Circle the name of each shape.

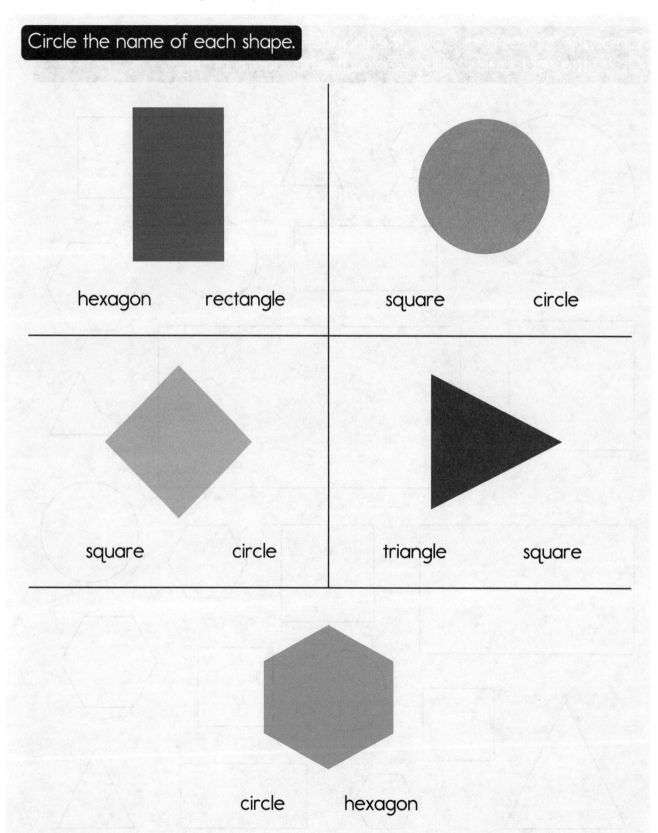

hexagon   rectangle

square   circle

square   circle

triangle   square

circle   hexagon

Name _____

Lesson 5.12 Naming Shapes

cone   sphere

cone   cylinder

cone   cube

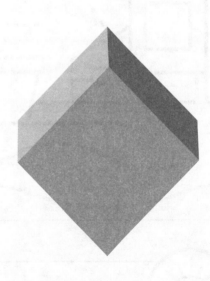

cylinder   cube

Name _____

Lesson 5.13 Drawing Shapes

Trace the circle and color it yellow. Trace the triangle and color it red. Color the rest of the scene.

 Draw a square under the sailboat.

Spectrum Math **Kindergarten**

Lesson 5.13 Drawing Shapes

Trace the rectangle and color it yellow. Trace the square and color it black. Trace the hexagon and color it red. Color the rest of the scene.

Lesson 5.14 Problem Solving: Finding Shapes

Color the triangles red. Color the rectangles blue. Color the circle yellow. Color the square green.

Name _____

Lesson 5.14 Problem Solving: Finding Shapes

Color the triangle red. Color the rectangles blue. Color the circle yellow. Color the square green.

Lesson 5.15 Tracing and Drawing Shapes

Trace the shape.

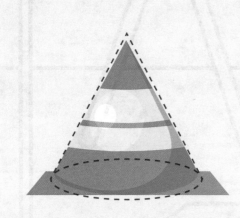

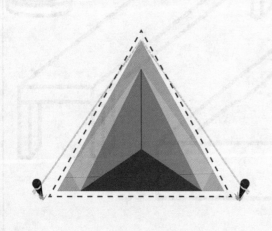

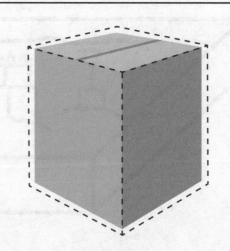

Name _____

Lesson 5.16 Composing Shapes

Combine the following shapes. Trace the shape you get.

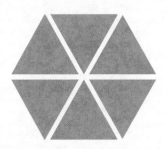 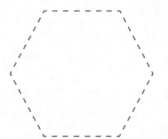

 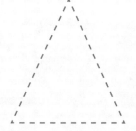

 How many shapes did
you need to create
each new shape? _____

Lesson 5.16 Composing Shapes

Follow the directions.

Make and draw a shape using 2 △s.

Make and draw a shape using 3 △s.

Make and draw a shape using 6 △s.

Write a number. Make and draw a shape using that number of △s.

_____

Lesson 5.16 Composing Shapes

Circle the group of shapes that make each hexagon. Draw the shapes inside the hexagon.

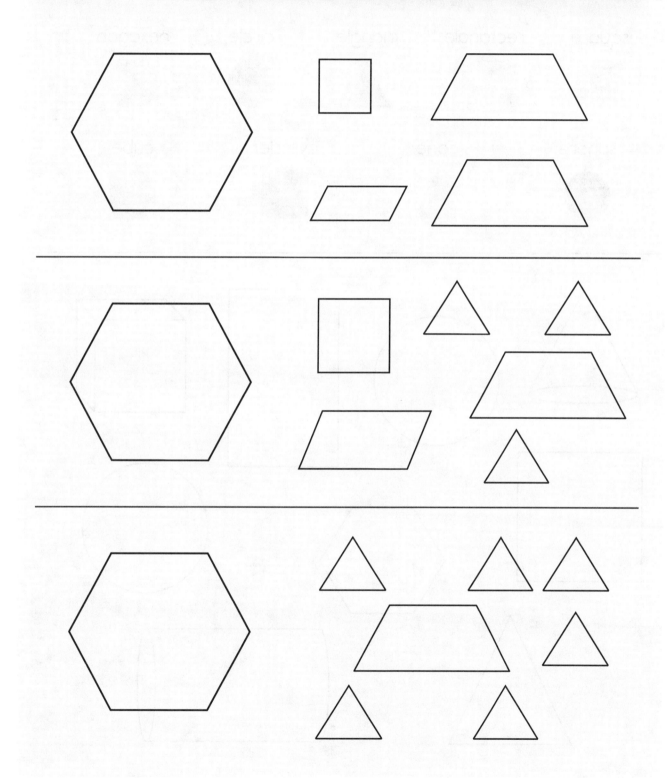

Review Chapter 5

Color the shapes to match the shapes at the top of the page. Circle all of the 2-D shapes. Mark an X on all of the 3-D shapes.

square   rectangle   triangle   circle   hexagon

sphere   cone   cylinder   cube

Spectrum Math **Kindergarten**

Name _____

Review Chapter 5

Color the circles yellow. Color the rectangles blue. Color the spheres
red. Color the triangle green. Color the cube gray.
Draw a circle above the rocket. Draw a triangle next to the rocket.
Draw a square below the rocket. Finish coloring the picture.

Learning Checkpoint Chapters 3–5

 Add.

$$\begin{array}{r} 3 \\ +\ 4 \\ \hline \end{array}$$

$$\begin{array}{r} 6 \\ +\ 4 \\ \hline \end{array}$$

$$\begin{array}{r} 7 \\ +\ 2 \\ \hline \end{array}$$

$$\begin{array}{r} 8 \\ +\ 1 \\ \hline \end{array}$$

Annika saw 5 shooting stars. Carol saw 3 shooting stars. How many shooting stars did they see in all?

_____

Learning Checkpoint Chapters 3–5

Subtract.

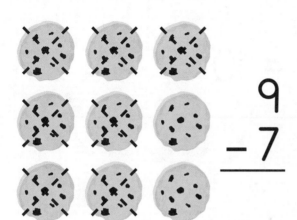

$$\begin{array}{r} 9 \\ -\,7 \\ \hline \end{array}$$

$$\begin{array}{r} 6 \\ -\,4 \\ \hline \end{array}$$

$$\begin{array}{r} 3 \\ -\,3 \\ \hline \end{array}$$

$$\begin{array}{r} 8 \\ -\,2 \\ \hline \end{array}$$

There are 6 kids playing at a park.
4 of the kids go home. How many
kids are left playing at the park?

_____

Learning Checkpoint Chapters 3–5

Count the total number of objects. Write the number that makes 10.

$$7 + \underline{\quad} = 10$$

$$10 = \underline{\quad} + 4$$

Circle the taller object.

Circle the lighter object.

Name _____

Learning Checkpoint Chapters 3–5

How many? Write the number.

_____ _____

Trace each shape. Draw each shape.

Learning Checkpoint Chapters 3–5

Circle the squares.

Circle the triangles.

Circle the cones.

Circle the cubes.

Name _____

Final Test

Circle the number.

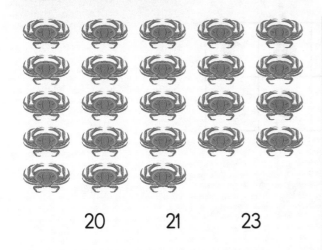

| 20 | 21 | 23 |

| 7 | 9 | 6 |

Count how many. Write the number.

_____

_ _ _ _ _

_____

_____

_ _ _ _ _

_____

Final Test

Draw dots to show 12.

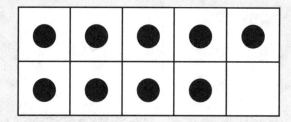

Draw dots to show 15.

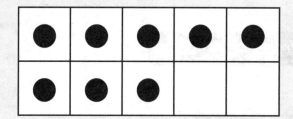

Write the missing numbers.

| 11 | |

| 5 | |

| | 9 |

| | 19 |

| 16 | | 18 |

| 19 | | 21 |

Name _____

Final Test

Count the objects in the first set. Color the set that is greater red. Color the set that is less yellow. If there is a set that is the same, or equal, color it blue.

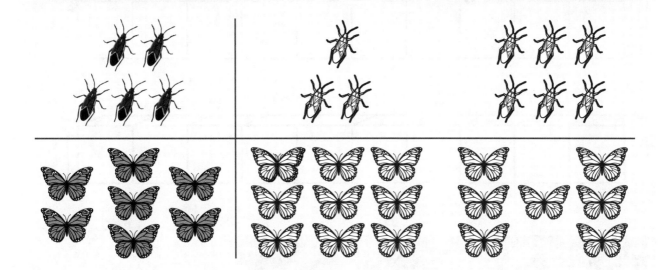

Circle the number that is greater.

10   9 | 3   5

Circle the number that is less.

2   1 | 7   4

Final Test

Use two colors to show the number 10 in two ways.

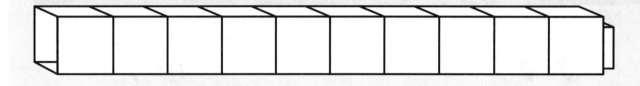

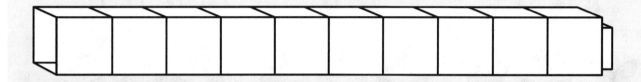

Write the missing number in each number bond.

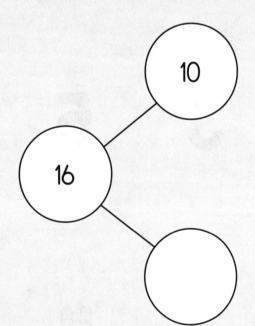

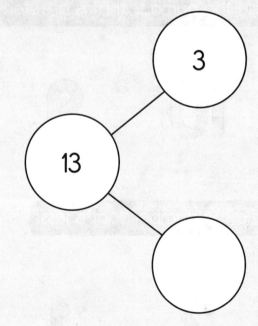

Spectrum Math **Kindergarten**

Final Test

Look at the pictures. Write the numbers to complete the addition number sentences.

_____ + _____ = 6

_____ + _____ = 10

Write the subtraction number sentence for each picture.

_____ – _____ = _____

_____ – _____ = _____

Name _____

Final Test

 Add.

There are 4 cats in a tree and 2 more cats join them. How many cats are in the tree in all?

 + = _____ cats

A farmer has 5 goats. She buys 3 more. How many goats does the farmer have now?

+ = _____ goats

Subtract.

There are 9 ants on the branch. Then, 2 ants fall off. How many ants are left on the branch?

= _____ ants

There are 7 birds in the birdhouse. Then, 3 birds fly away. How many birds are left in the birdhouse?

= _____ birds

Spectrum Math **Kindergarten**

Name _____

Final Test

Circle the word that best describes each object.

light heavy

light heavy

short tall

short tall

Circle the word that describes how each object compares to the ruler.

longer shorter

longer shorter

Final Test

Circle the word that describes how each object compares to the whale.

lighter   heavier   lighter   heavier

How many? Write the number.

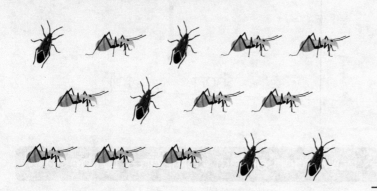 

_____ _____

_____ _____ _____

Final Test

Circle the name of each shape. Color the 2-D shapes red. Color the 3-D shapes blue.

circle cylinder	rectangle square
sphere square	triangle cone
cube square	circle square
triangle cone	cone rectangle
triangle cone	hexagon rectangle

Final Test

Use a word from the word bank to complete each sentence.

above	behind	in
in front of	under	

 The bird is _____ the nest.

 The bird is _____ the nest.

 The bird is _____ the nest.

 The bird is _____ the nest.

 The bird is _____ the nest.

Answer Key

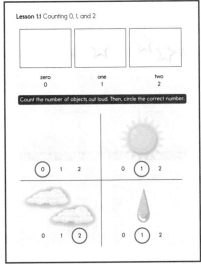

page 8

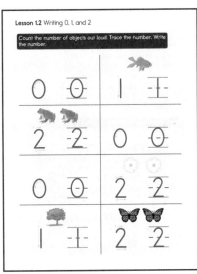

page 9

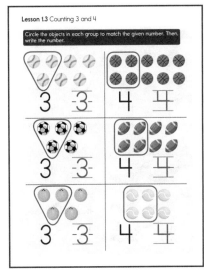

page 10

page 11

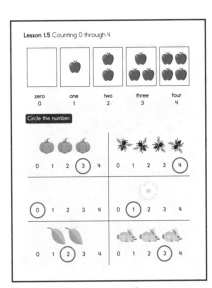

page 12

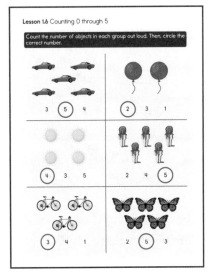

page 13

Answer Key

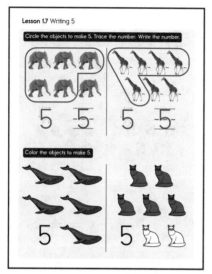

page 14

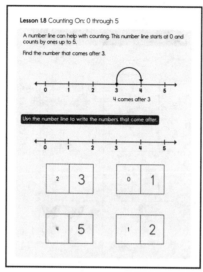

page 15

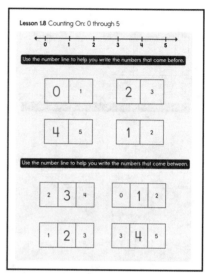

page 16

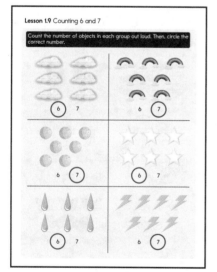

page 17

page 18

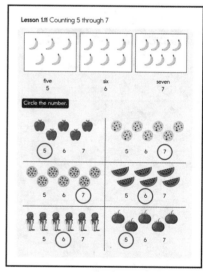

page 19

Answer Key

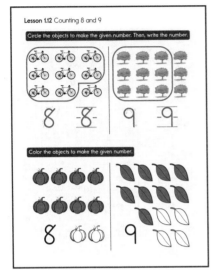

page 20

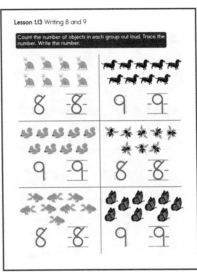

page 21

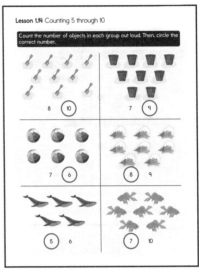

page 22

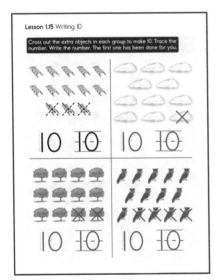

page 23

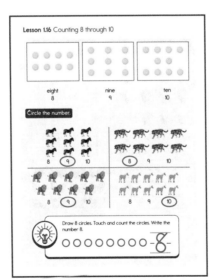

page 24

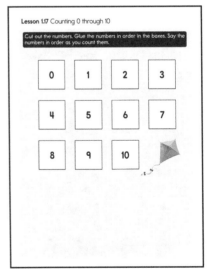

page 25

Answer Key

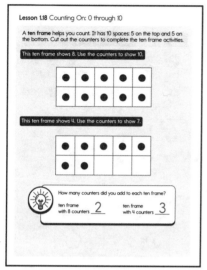

page 27

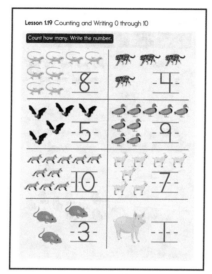

page 29

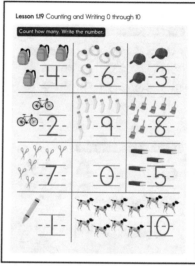

page 30

page 31

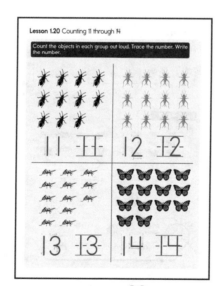

page 32

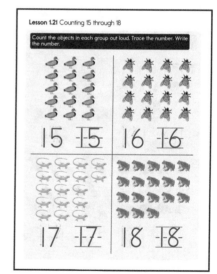

page 33

Spectrum Math **Kindergarten**

Answer Key

page 34

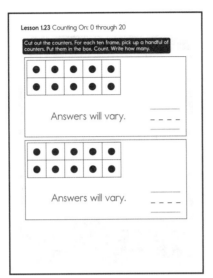

page 35

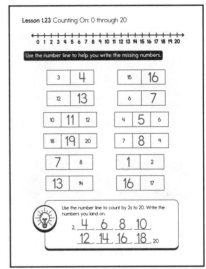

page 37

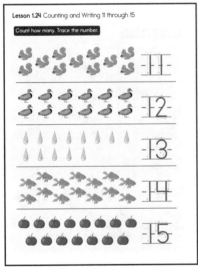

page 38

page 39

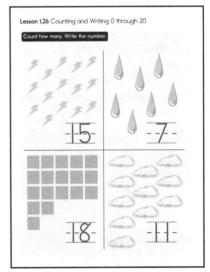

page 40

Answer Key

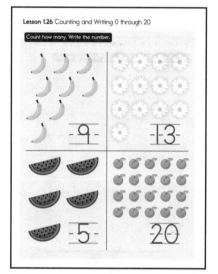

page 41

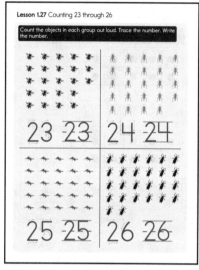

page 42

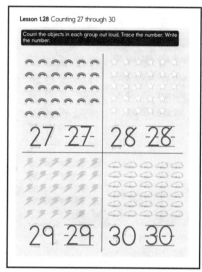

page 43

page 44

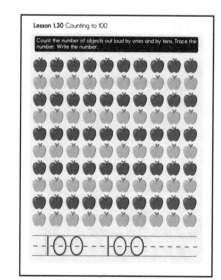

page 45

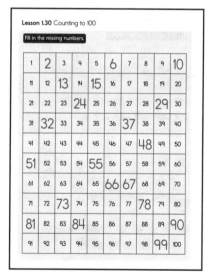

page 46

Answer Key

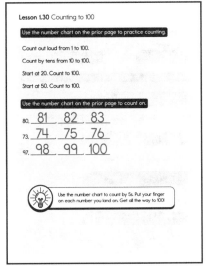

page 47

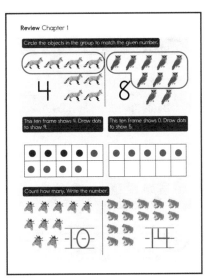

page 48

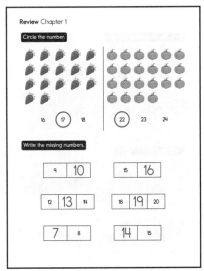

page 49

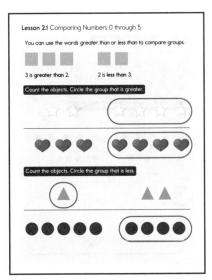

page 52

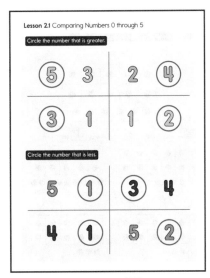

page 53

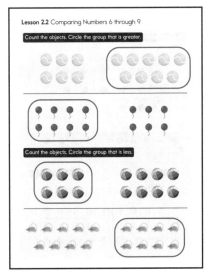

page 54

Answer Key

page 55

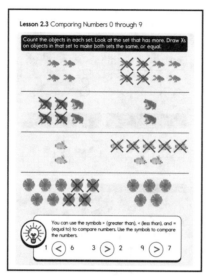

page 56

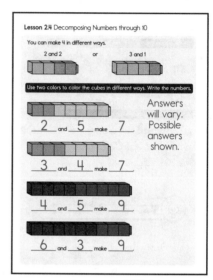

page 57

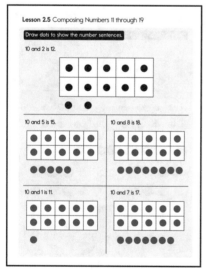

page 58

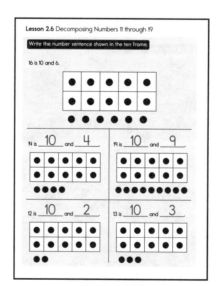

page 59

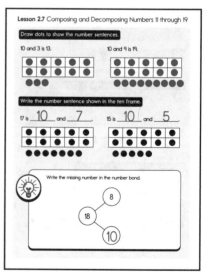

page 60

Answer Key

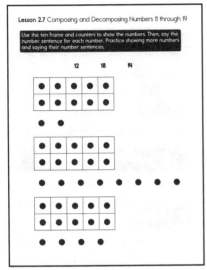

page 61

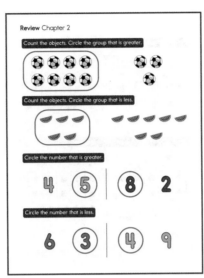

page 63

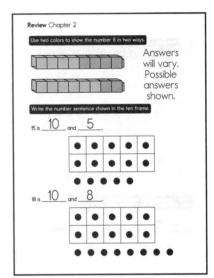

page 64

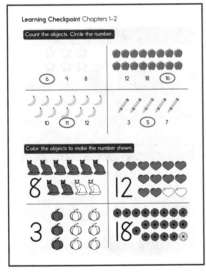

page 65

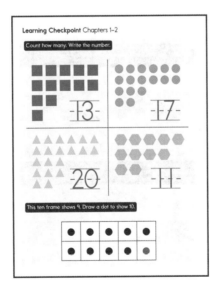

page 66

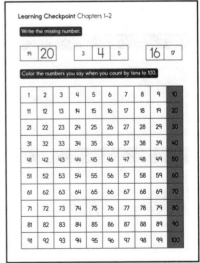

page 67

Answer Key

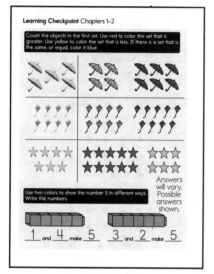

page 68

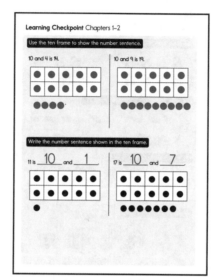

page 69

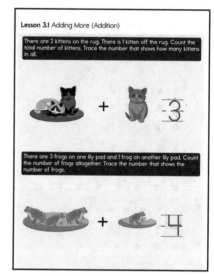

page 72

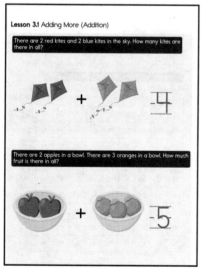

page 73

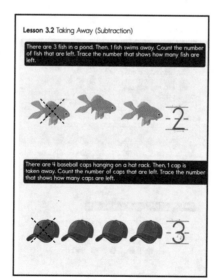

page 74

page 75

172

Answer Key

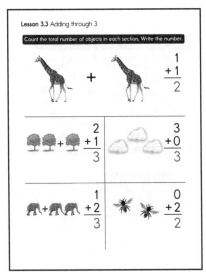

page 76

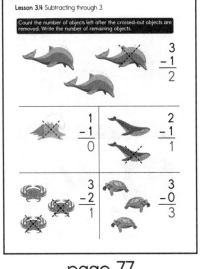

page 77

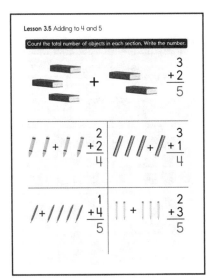

page 78

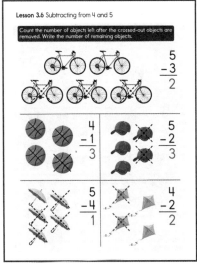

page 79

Answer Key

page 80

page 81

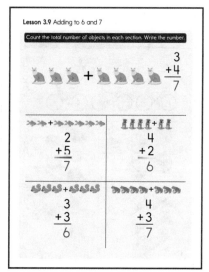

page 82

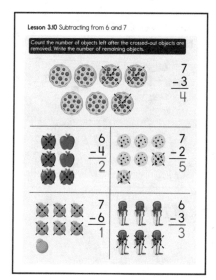

page 83

Answer Key

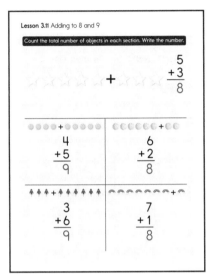

page 84

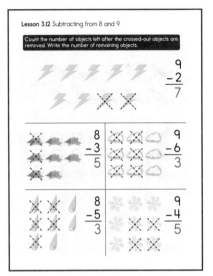

page 85

Lesson 3.13 Making 10

Count the total number of objects in each set. Circle the number that makes 10.

6 + ___ = 10   1   (4)   2

___ + 3 = 10   10 = 8 + ___

5   (7)   4   3   5   (2)

___ + 5 = 10   10 = 9 + ___

(5)   8   9   4   7   (1)

page 86

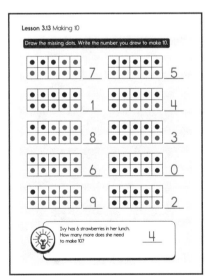

page 87

Answer Key

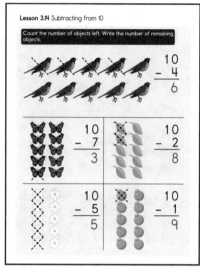

page 88

Lesson 3.15 Adding Numbers

Add.

$$\begin{array}{r} 3 \\ +3 \\ \hline 6 \end{array} \qquad \begin{array}{r} 4 \\ +2 \\ \hline 6 \end{array}$$

$$\begin{array}{r} 8 \\ +2 \\ \hline 10 \end{array} \qquad \begin{array}{r} 5 \\ +3 \\ \hline 8 \end{array}$$

$$\begin{array}{r} 3 \\ +6 \\ \hline 9 \end{array} \qquad \begin{array}{r} 7 \\ +1 \\ \hline 8 \end{array}$$

page 89

Lesson 3.15 Adding Numbers

Add.

$$\begin{array}{r} 3 \\ +2 \\ \hline 5 \end{array} \qquad \begin{array}{r} 3 \\ +1 \\ \hline 4 \end{array}$$

$$\begin{array}{r} 0 \\ +5 \\ \hline 5 \end{array} \qquad \begin{array}{r} 1 \\ +1 \\ \hline 2 \end{array}$$

$$\begin{array}{r} 2 \\ +2 \\ \hline 4 \end{array} \qquad \begin{array}{r} 4 \\ +1 \\ \hline 5 \end{array}$$

page 90

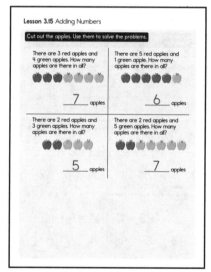

page 91

Answer Key

Lesson 3.15 Adding Numbers

Write a number sentence to help you solve each problem.

Amir saw 5 birds. Jada saw 1 bird. How many birds did they see in all?

$$\underline{5} + \underline{1} = \underline{6} \text{ birds}$$

Kiara has 3 fish. Deja has 4 fish. How many fish do they have in all?

$$\underline{3} + \underline{4} = \underline{7} \text{ fish}$$

Mei kicked 2 balls. Finn kicked 6 balls. How many balls did they kick in all?

$$\underline{2} + \underline{6} = \underline{8} \text{ balls}$$

Hiro drew 6 pictures. Eve drew 3 pictures. How many pictures did they draw in all?

$$\underline{6} + \underline{3} = \underline{9} \text{ pictures}$$

page 93

Lesson 3.16 Subtracting Numbers

Subtract.

$$\begin{array}{r} 8 \\ -3 \\ \hline 5 \end{array} \qquad \begin{array}{r} 9 \\ -9 \\ \hline 0 \end{array}$$

$$\begin{array}{r} 5 \\ -2 \\ \hline 3 \end{array} \qquad \begin{array}{r} 7 \\ -5 \\ \hline 2 \end{array}$$

$$\begin{array}{r} 6 \\ -3 \\ \hline 3 \end{array} \qquad \begin{array}{r} 10 \\ -5 \\ \hline 5 \end{array}$$

page 94

Lesson 3.16 Subtracting Numbers

Subtract.

$$\begin{array}{r} 3 \\ -2 \\ \hline 1 \end{array} \qquad \begin{array}{r} 2 \\ -1 \\ \hline 1 \end{array}$$

$$\begin{array}{r} 1 \\ -1 \\ \hline 0 \end{array} \qquad \begin{array}{r} 4 \\ -2 \\ \hline 2 \end{array}$$

$$\begin{array}{r} 3 \\ -0 \\ \hline 3 \end{array} \qquad \begin{array}{r} 4 \\ -3 \\ \hline 1 \end{array}$$

page 95

Lesson 3.16 Subtracting Numbers

Write a number sentence to help you solve each problem.

Gia has 6 cookies. She eats 1 cookie. How many cookies does Gia have left?

$$\underline{6} - \underline{1} = \underline{5} \text{ cookies}$$

Hasan has 7 flowers. He gives 6 flowers to his grandma. How many flowers does Hasan have left?

$$\underline{7} - \underline{6} = \underline{1} \text{ flowers}$$

Nadia has 8 coins. She loses 4 coins. How many coins does Nadia have left?

$$\underline{8} - \underline{4} = \underline{4} \text{ coins}$$

Ryder has 9 cherries. He eats 7 cherries. How many cherries does Ryder have left?

$$\underline{9} - \underline{7} = \underline{2} \text{ cherries}$$

page 96

Answer Key

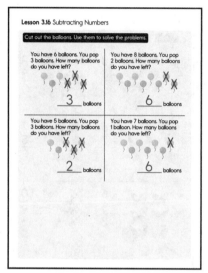

page 97

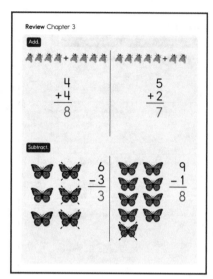

page 99

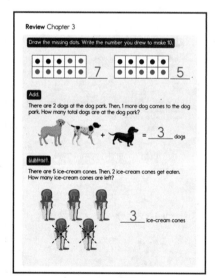

page 100

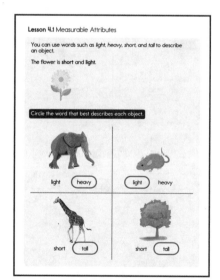

page 102

Answer Key

Lesson 4.1 Measurable Attributes

Complete each sentence. Draw a picture.

I am lighter than _____

_____.

I am heavier than _____

_____.

Sentences and drawings will vary.

I am shorter than _____

_____.

I am taller than _____

_____.

page 103

Lesson 4.2 Longer and Shorter

Color the shorter object in each row green. Color the longer object blue. The first one has been done for you.

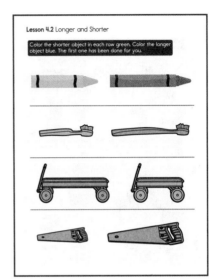

page 104

Lesson 4.3 Describing an Object

Circle the word that describes how each object compares to the paperclip.

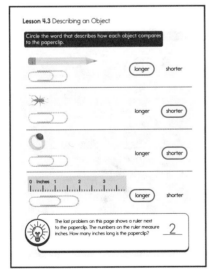

longer   shorter

longer   shorter

longer   shorter

longer   shorter

The last problem on this page shows a ruler next to the paperclip. The numbers on the ruler measure inches. How many inches long is the paperclip?   2

page 105

Lesson 4.4 Taller and Shorter

Circle the taller object in each section. Draw an X on the shorter object.

Draw an animal that is taller than the cat. Number the cat, mouse, and your drawing from shortest (1) to tallest (3).

Answers will vary.

page 106

Answer Key

page 107

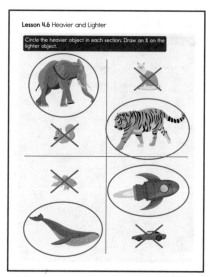

page 108

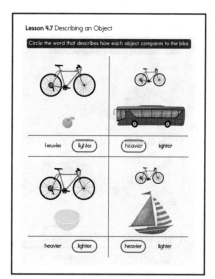

page 109

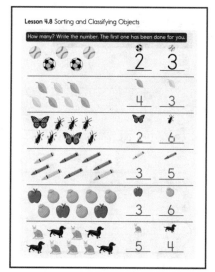

page 110

Answer Key

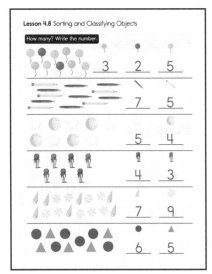

page 111

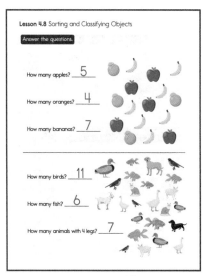

page 112

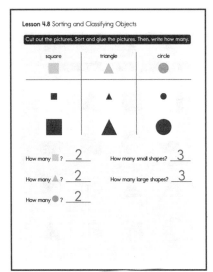

page 113

page 115

Answer Key

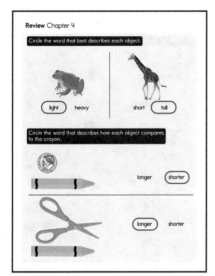

page 116

page 117

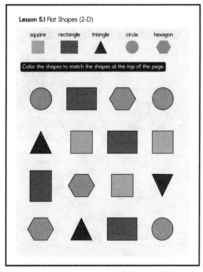

page 120

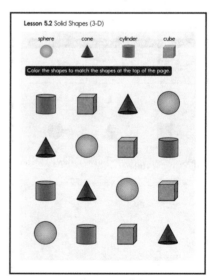

page 121

Answer Key

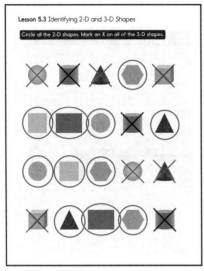

page 122

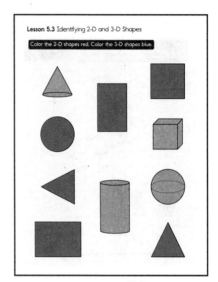

page 123

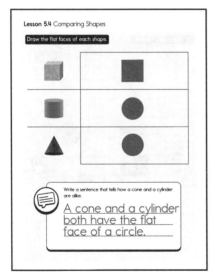

page 124

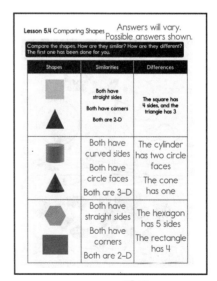

page 125

Answer Key

page 126

page 127

page 129

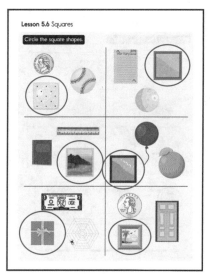

page 130

Answer Key

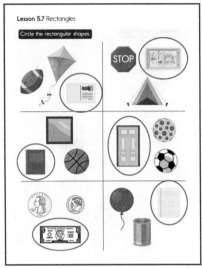

page 131

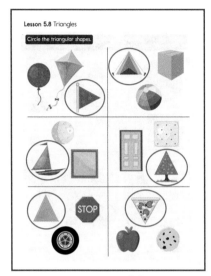

page 132

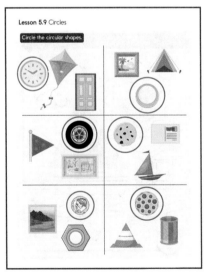

page 133

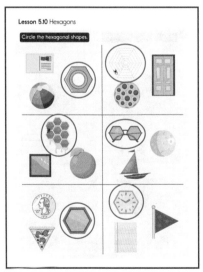

page 134

Answer Key

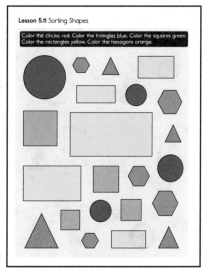

page 135

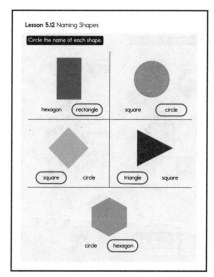

page 136

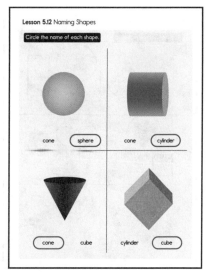

page 137

page 138

Answer Key

page 139

page 140

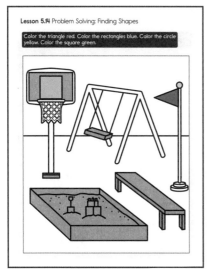

page 141

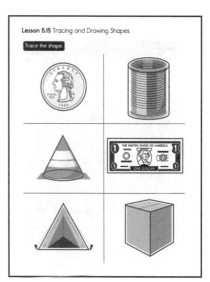

page 142

Answer Key

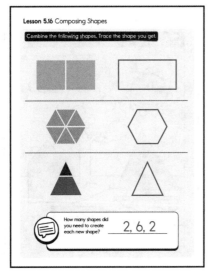

page 143

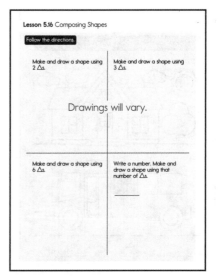

page 144

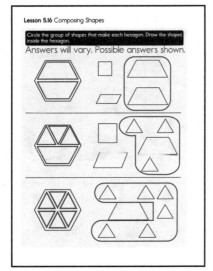

page 145

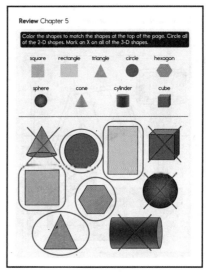

page 146

Answer Key

page 147

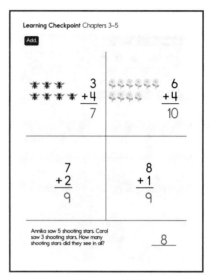

page 148

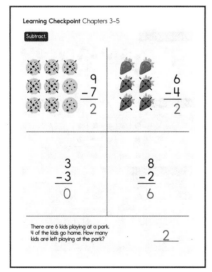

page 149

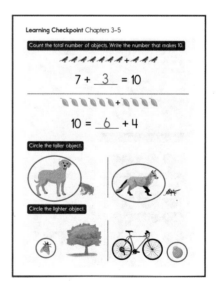

page 150

Answer Key

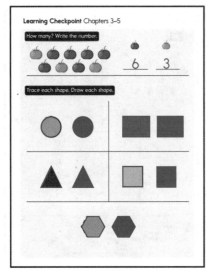

page 151

page 152

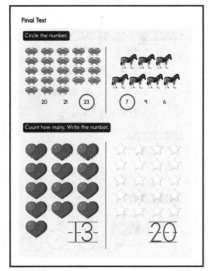

page 153

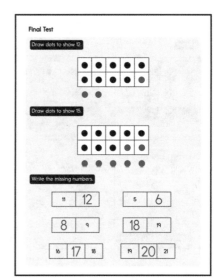

page 154

Answer Key

page 155

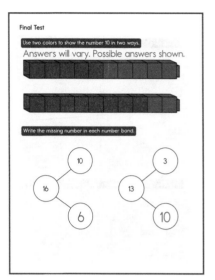

page 156

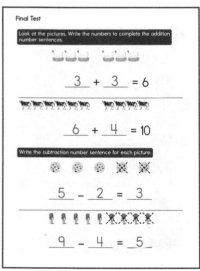

page 157

Final Test

Add.

There are 4 cats in a tree and 2 more cats join them. How many cats are in the tree in all?

= __6__ cats

A farmer has 5 goats. She buys 3 more. How many goats does the farmer have now?

= __8__ goats

Subtract.

There are 9 ants on the branch. Then, 2 ants fall off. How many ants are left on the branch?

= __7__ ants

There are 7 birds in the birdhouse. Then, 3 birds fly away. How many birds are left in the birdhouse?

= __4__ birds

page 158

Answer Key

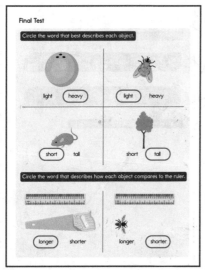

page 159

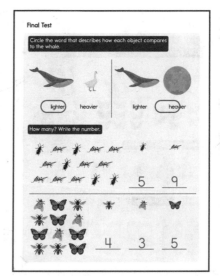

page 160

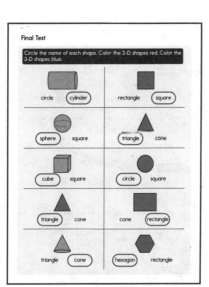

page 161

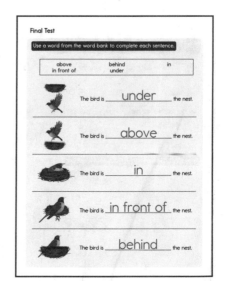

page 162

Spectrum Math **Kindergarten**